MW01613251

THE GRAND FACADE

How your emotions shape you and how releasing them allows you to reshape yourself!

Danielle Gaucher

Copyright © 2022 Danielle Gaucher

All rights reserved. No part of this publication may be reproduced, distributed, or transmitted in any form or by any means, including photocopying, recording, or other electronic, or mechanical methods, without the prior written permission of the author or publisher, except in the case of brief quotations embodied in reviews and certain other non-commercial uses permitted by copyright law.

This publication is designed to provide accurate and authoritative information regarding the subject matter covered. It is sold with the understanding that the author or publisher is not engaged in rendering legal, accounting, or other professional services. If legal advice or other expert assistance is required, the services of a competent professional person should be sought.

ISBN: 978-1-7387329-0-6

Printed in Canada and the United States of America

"…..*And the grand facade, so soon will burn. Without a noise, and without my pride, I reach out from the inside.*"

~ PETER GABRIEL, IN YOUR EYES.

"This book is dedicated to whomever chooses to read it. Personal work is hard. Avoiding personal work is hard. Thank you for choosing the hard that honours the truth of who you've always been. ~ Danielle"

YOUR FREE GIFT

As a huge thank you for buying my book, I wanted to help you further by providing you with an activity guide that provides you with additional exercises and thoughts to help you process your own experiences as you read through this book.

You can grab your copy here:
https://www.yourconnectioncoach.ca

FOREWORD

It has been my pleasure to have worked with Danielle since 2014, supporting her on her healing journey.

I am very impressed with how far she has come and how committed and determined she is to be the best person she can possibly be.

This book is a true testimonial to a courageous woman's struggles and healing. It takes so much vulnerability to be willing to share to this level and I'm sure that this book will touch many hearts.

The theory is available to anyone who desires it, but not everyone dives head first into changing their lives for the better as Danielle has done.

~ Susan Aaron, *Ontario Registered Psychotherapist, Canadian certified director of Psychodrama, and creator of the training program Psychodramatic Bodywork®. You can learn more about Susan at* www.youremotions.com.

TABLE OF CONTENTS

PROLOGUE

"Drive the car, Danielle!"

Just as I neared the end of our street, I saw our youngest son riding his bike toward us.

"Your brother's in the house," I said to him. "Put your bike away, and head inside. Dad and I are heading out, and I'll let you both know when we'll be back."

I have no idea how I put that sentence together. It was like forces beyond me took over, and put my speech together for me. I had no idea when we would be back.

"Drive the car, Danielle!"

"... My husband is forty four, his brother died of a heart attack at forty three, and I think he's having a heart attack. Please be ready for us when we get there!"

This is what I heard myself telling the emergency department of our local hospital, to which I was enroute.

The voice responded, telling me Jeff would be assessed when we arrived, and seen in order of priority. I heard myself cutting her off like a machete would a blade of grass.

"My husband is forty four, his brother died of a heart attack at fourty three, and I think he's having a heart attack!! He is a PRIORITY!!"

After hanging up with the hospital, Jeff spoke for the first time since we got in the car. I had stopped at a set of lights. He threw a monotone dart my way: "Drive through the fucking lights."

I couldn't believe what I was hearing. I was *terrified* but there was no time to feel it.

"Drive the car, Danielle!"

"I'm gonna pass out." He seemed to be forcing the words out.

I set my hand on his leg, "Just close your eyes and breathe, hon. I'm going to get you to the hospital, I promise." I had *no* idea where those words of comfort came from. They were the last words we would share before his heart stopped. I heard a *thud.* I couldn't look.

"Drive the car, Danielle! Drive the car, Danielle!"

Time seemed to slow at this point. I wish it hadn't. There would be less space to hold the memories. I wanted this to be a dream. I wanted to wake up. I was forced to slam on the brakes as the light was turning from yellow to red, and another car had entered the intersection. The abrupt stop forced Jeff's lifeless body forward, then back. I looked just as Jeff's head flew back. His lifeless gray eyes met mine. I was alone.

"He's *gone*...he's had a heart attack." I couldn't believe what I heard myself saying. "Oh my God, Oh my God, Oh my God!" I must have said more, but that's all I recall.

Do I pull over? Do I pull Jeff out of the car and start CPR? Do I keep driving?

Then I heard myself again, ***"Drive the car, Danielle."***

When the emergency doors opened, time slowed again. I watched as a team of hospital staff flocked to Jeff's aid like the perfect football huddle. They seemed to be moving in slow motion. I could see their mouths moving, offering direction to each other, but the sounds were muffled in my ears. They pulled him out of the car. He was missing a shoe. They started CPR right there on the concrete, outside the emergency doors.

Loaded onto a gurney, the emergency nurse rode the stretcher through the automatic doors as she continued CPR on Jeff. The doors shut behind him, and I was alone again. I stood there, the passenger side door still open. Jeff's other shoe was visible. I was asked to move my car. "Move my car? I don't remember how to drive," I muttered to a security guard standing there. He came with me for support.

I raced across the parking lot on foot. I felt like I was floating when I entered the emergency doors through which Jeff's lifeless body had disappeared. A nurse met me and led me right to Jeff. I watched as the medical team worked vigorously on him.

"All clear!"

I heard that two or three times; or was it six or seven times?? Whatever the number, I knew it was bad. My fear of just how bad it was, was confirmed when my sister came flying through that same set of emergency doors. Tina lived twenty-five minutes away. She was at home when we arrived. At that moment, I knew Jeff's heart had stopped more than twenty-five minutes earlier.

"This is really bad isn't it, Sis?" I could always trust my sister to be honest and supportive.

"Yes it is."

Her answer felt like a ten tonne weight crushing my chest.

Time hasn't slowed down.

I felt nothing, and everything, all at once. There was a feeling of familiarity. Where had I felt this before? I stood fixated on my husband's lifeless shell; I could feel my heart racing. I knew my legs were shaking.

In that moment, it's as if Jeff and I were standing on opposite ends of a lifeline continuum. Jeff: leaving his body. Me: landing in mine. I was present. I hadn't run. It was like each defib administered a shock into Jeff's heart, and into my essence; in unison. I was experiencing the most bizarre dichotomy of Jeff leaving his body, and me coming back into mine.

CHAPTER 1: THE SMILE

I think I've been afraid for most of my life. Fear took up so much space in my body, that there was little room left for me. The story I told myself at a young age was that something was wrong with me and that the world was a scary place. I brilliantly navigated this narrative by creating roles and by wearing costumes to fit each role like a suit of armour. Every role was another layer that helped me develop, what I believed to be, a sense of safety and control. The layers helped me hide my fear from the adults in my life. As an adult I was able to hide my fear from both the world, and myself. No one knew how scared I was, least of all me. What began to happen later in life as I developed self-awareness, was a realization that the tactics I was using may have fooled the world, and even my own mind; but my body was never fooled. **My body *endured*, until it could no longer.**

 "There's no place like home." This is perhaps the most famous line spoken by the character Dorothy in one of my daughter's favourite movies, "The Wizard of Oz." To me, it connotes the feeling of warmth and familiarity experienced in the safety of one's home.

But what if your experience of home *wasn't* one of warmth and safety? What if your first experience of the place you called home was one of isolation and fear? What if I told you that from as far back as I can remember, *I* have little recollection of home being a place of warmth and security?

Instead, I remember fear. I could feel it all around me. And I could feel it *in* my body. I suppose that makes sense, because what is memory, if not the recollection of feelings? I don't have, after all, a conscious memory of the time spent in my mother's womb. I have only the feelings that unconsciously nourished my developing sense of self. In many ways, I believe that I was nurtured in an environment of fear. I'll go as far as to say that, even in the womb, the environment in which I was developing must have been a scary place, riddled with anxiety and fear.

I am a rainbow baby, which is best described as a healthy baby who's born after the loss of a child due to neonatal death, infant loss, miscarriage, or still birth. Prior to my arrival, my mom gave birth to my older sister, and then four years later, gave birth to a full-term baby who died during childbirth. She was a girl, and my mom had named her Nadine.

My mom was overwhelmed with trauma, and she suffered in silence. She was unable to grieve her tragic loss. That's obvious to me today, because when I ask her about Nadine, she responds with tears rather than words. Her tears seem to come quickly, and get sucked back even faster. Her grief sits center stage, behind a drawn curtain, always prepared for the curtain to open and a spotlight to illuminate that grief.

For my mom, the option to feel, to explore, and to heal her trauma never existed. My mother was married to a verbally and physically abusive man. He was an alcoholic and he abused prescription drugs. She still refers to him as her first love. He was a police officer who abused his power in the community and perhaps more so in the home. I imagine this to be why she holds back her tears so well. I can understand that as a mother myself, not wanting to cry in front of *my own* children. How different would both of our stories be if she had been able to express, and be held in her grief?

My mom's story is hers to tell, and not mine. But what I can share from a place of personal and professional experience **about intimate partner violence is that an abuser is, first and foremost, seeking power and control.** My biological father buried Nadine while my mom was still in the hospital. My mom was never afforded the space or the dignity to honour Nadine in ritual or in ceremony. You see, **an abuser will always find the most effective way to gain and maintain power and control in a relationship, denying the victim the love and connection they so desire, and deserve.** My mom was informed that the baby had been buried, and not another word was spoken about her. When she returned to the marital home, Nadine's room was empty as if the space that had been lovingly created for her, by my mom, had never existed. There was no space for grief. No compassion. No room.

Having given birth to five healthy children myself, I can't begin to imagine the pain and grief of my mother's loss. I'm convinced my mother lost even more than a child back then. I imagine a piece of my mother died then too. I've never experienced the loss of a child. I think if I had, I too would lose a part of myself in their death. My mom returned home to my older sister who was nearly four years old, in a home where she felt silenced and powerless.

RESOURCE SUGGESTION

The Power and Control Wheel. This wheel was birthed from a Domestic Abuse Project out of Duluth, Minnesota in 1984. I also encourage using the crisis line of your local Women and Children's Shelter if you, or someone you know, suspects they are in an abusive relationship.

Its no surprise to me, nor will it be to you as you read on, that I've spent over 20 years working in the Violence Against Women sector in my community. I can still recall the feeling that washed over me when I first walked through the doors of the shelter. Back then, I would have told you that I was nervous and excited and so hopeful to be chosen as a volunteer. I was truly stunned when I was hired, rather than placed on the volunteer roster.

If you asked my mom if she was surprised, she would say something like, "Not at all! Danielle is incredibly selfless, humble and wise."

What I know to be true today, however, as I share the story of my first home with you, is that there was a feeling of familiarity at the shelter. I'd never lived in a shelter before, yet I had a sense of returning to a space I knew well.

What I realize all these years later is the feeling of familiarity I encountered upon walking through those shelter doors. It was the feeling of fear. I was home. And "there's no place like home," right? Especially when all you know is fear. I still recall the visceral feeling.

It takes incredible courage to leave your home and go to a shelter for safety. Women overcome unimaginable barriers daily in our communities, and across the country accessing shelter supports to break the cycle of violence in their lives. They seem to move wearing survival vests coated with terror and wisdom. From the first woman I spoke with at the dining table in the shelter, I was in awe of women's resilience and ability to navigate the abuse and trauma in their lives. It made sense to me that I'd landed, that I was on the right professional path, that I'd secured employment that matched my skill set and passion for helping others. My body, however, told me I was moving into a home just like that of my mother's womb.

Just one year after my mom lost Nadine, I was born. My mom has described her pregnancy with me as riddled with anxiety, fear and unexpressed grief. She secretly grieved Nadine while fearing she might not carry me to full term. She continued to experience abuse at the hands of my biological father, worked full time as a teacher, and raised my older sister, Tina, in as safe a manner as she could. All the while, as a baby in the womb, I was growing amidst the emotional frequencies that echoed within my mother's body.

My mom has since shared that her self worth was low, and she did all she could to keep my sister safe. She was afraid of the abuse she would face if she tried to leave the marriage. She knew that her husband was capable of violence. After all, she was married to an abusive police officer in the seventies, and that meant that my mother faced additional barriers to leaving. **She knew he had easy access to weapons; and he reminded her of this. If she left it would get worse. She knew this.**

RESOURCE SUGGESTION

Book: When Love Hurts: A Woman's Guide to Understanding Abuse in Relationships by Jill Cory and Karen McAndless-Davis.

Telling this story gives me a deeper understanding of how my mom accepted what became *my normal* growing up: "What happens behind closed doors, stays behind closed doors."

These particular doors were like a gateway from 'The Neverending Story'; guarded by the two sphinxes who were ready to shoot lasers at anyone who dared pass through, showing fear.

My mom kept herself isolated and alone at that time, keeping the abuse in her marriage a secret. She questioned her safety and that of her family if ever she had the nerve to seek help to leave. So my mom endured. She did this with courage and strength. I was learning from the embryonic stage that the world was unsafe, but she must have been terrified. How did she put on a brave and joyful face for all of her students each day? How exhausted her cheeks and jaw must have been at the end of each school day holding that smile. I wonder if any co-worker knew the narrative she held behind her gated smile?

There's a real dichotomy in the role of the smile, isn't there? This facial gesture can both pull folks in, and keep them away. Flashing the pearly whites may offer an invitation, or act as a repellent to connections. I know I have used *the smile*, combined with statements like, "I'm fine" and, "no thanks, I'm good" to keep my vulnerability a secret.

The smile kept my fear, and all of my emotions encased. It was as if my body became a cabinet; my organs and parts like vials of pain I was filling to the brim. If I could just hold my smile; the picture told the only story I believed I was equipped to tell.

There was, however, a peeping Tom doing a dance outside my *closed doors* like a child outside a bathroom stall. This *interruptor* wasn't terribly intrusive when I was younger. He became more bothersome as I got older. The interrupter was named, "injury." It became like a wartime carrier pigeon; each break or surgery provided new information that took me back to reset my plan of attack. My goal was to stay on course; lead with a smile, and show no weakness. My plan began to fail despite incredible medical care. Like a car taking several bangs off a guard rail, I had been permanently thrown off alignment.

I decided to put my story in a book to further explore how I've navigated trauma in the past, and evaluate how I'm healing. I wanted to honour my story. I'm hoping that sharing it encourages anyone who reads even one paragraph, to consider honouring their story. Just weeks into writing this book, I read the beginning of it to my mom and sister. My voice trembled as I read. I stuttered here and there. I needed to take deep breaths, but pushed through. When I was finished, I looked up from my laptop and met my mother's eyes.

My mom has a presence that fills a room like a bouquet of fragrant flowers. One might think with deep purple streaks in her hair, that would be the first place your eyes would go when you meet her. It isn't; it's her smile. My mother's smile is like a kaleidoscope of joy. It's no wonder keeping the attention of students for over 25 years came easy to her.

As I looked into my mother's eyes, I could see her tears. Her smile had vanished. I sat and stared. She stared back. She gave me *the smile*, and it has served me incredibly well. I am grateful for her for giving me a life, giving me my sis, and for providing me the gift of infinite abilities. I am appreciative of the voice I have found today; the courage to share my childhood story with my Mom and Sis through *my* lense, from the living room of *my* home.

My sister, who sat beside me, seemed to know her place at this moment and was in silence. I'm wondering too, if she disappeared into *her* childhood as I read, and was taking the time she needed to ease back into the present. Perhaps like me, sharing the dialogue with our mom leading up to the reading felt strange. Tina and I only opened up to each other in our thirties about the realities and impact of our childhood traumas. Like my mom, my sister has a presence that is uniquely bright and welcoming. She, too, inherited *the smile*. She can be the life of the party; and in fact, she often *is* the party. She is stunning in appearance, and has truly captivating inner beauty. She is a mental health nurse and leads with relentless compassion. Her energy is something folks are drawn to, and the world is simply a better place with her in it.

I broke the stillness by standing up and walking over to my mom, with tears now reaching her cheeks. I stood over her, and held out my arms. I'm not mad at my mom, and I don't want to hurt her. I admire her strength and courage; perhaps more now than ever. She could have run away when I started to read. I wouldn't have judged her reaction at all. My mom slowly rose from the couch, and for the first time, I didn't question why my mother's body seemed to be out of alignment. It was as if I could actually see the weight of her years of emotional suppression and trauma having set like concrete in her joints.

Bringing forth a piece of our family story that had remained behind closed doors for most of my lifetime was surreal. It was also incredibly healing for all 3 of us. This narrative was cracking open the vault holding the stories we lived behind closed doors. It felt as if a heavy veil had been lifted. My mom hugged me so tight I could feel each of her 10 fingers gripping my back. I felt her chest rise and fall rapidly.

After a few moments, she whispered in my ear, "I'm so sorry I didn't keep you safe."

With my own tears now gliding down my face, I whispered back, "You weren't able to keep yourself safe."

All these years later, I can't help but marvel at the irony of being called a *rainbow baby;* my life as a child was anything but rainbow-like. Perhaps this planted a seed within me to create a safe role where I'd forever face the world with a smile. *The smile.*

To this day, most would describe my mother as, "Always happy and bubbly."

A smile is a powerful mask that's able to hide fear, sadness, and anger. A rainbow prompts images of pastels and sunshine, and yet, I felt largely void of colour. I'd be forced to pull colours from a very different palate in order to paint my story.

Rainbows appear after the storm. And it's a legend that there is a pot of gold at the end of every one of them. But I was born in the midst of a tsunami. Learning to present as always content, even cheerful, was a brilliant mask for the fear that was ever present in me. I feel like my DNA was infiltrated by fear; I was groomed to survive an emotional apocalypse where all that remained as sustenance was fear.

My birth, immersed in my mother's fear, was the lens through which I saw the world. Fear became my language; the identity hidden below my flesh and setting-up camp within my organs. I knew it so well. I have zero recollection of *not* knowing it. But I hid it so well, I forgot where it was, or that I even had it. Fear was all of me, and I denied its existence. And it was in this denial that I committed the ultimate betrayal: I abandoned myself. I abandoned myself both physically and emotionally.

A smile has played a powerful role in my family of origin. I learned that living my life behind a blanket of fear had come from the fearful homes where I grew up. I inherited *the smile* to mask my fear, and found it worked brilliantly as armour for protection *from*, and presentation *to* the world. Sharing my story throughout this book began with a conversation with my mother and sister. This dialogue offered healing and clarity; I could see my own pain in my mothers body, and feel inspired to continue to heal myself, and hold space for others to do the same.

"*Healing doesn't mean the damage never existed. It means the damage no longer controls our lives.*"

AKSHAY DUBEY

CHAPTER 2: JONESIN' FOR CONTROL

Looking back, I can see that I worked tirelessly; convincing myself and the world that I wasn't afraid. I built a vessel that consumed fear as fuel; yet, as the captain of my ship, I was pirated by self abandonment. I can still see that little girl who became a woman; both iterations lacking in self-awareness. I was a shell, forever waiting for the next scary story to inhabit my space, providing what I felt was purpose and meaning. The scariest stories had me rolling out the red carpet to welcome them. With open arms, I would greet fear and fill my body with the familiar energy of my first home in the womb. I navigated this fear vessel brilliantly; I kept her in a deep sea of silence as a young child. Being seen and not heard kept my outsides safe, while my insides festered with fear, confusion, shame and guilt.

As a teenager, I shifted out of stealth mode and plowed through like an icebreaker ship. I hated feeling so weak and helpless; I was growing to hate my constant state of vulnerability. I feel as if by the time I was a teenager I had a skewed perception of how to trust and be trusted, and love and be loved. I hated my fear, and I was growing a hatred for myself. I was scared and mad, which I later learned was the formula for blind rage. I'll speak on the cost to my sense of self, but in reflection, I recognize the value my rage afforded me. I felt seen, heard and safe in rage. Perhaps I was able to release just enough emotion in those blasts to ward off illness?

"Blind rage is like an extreme form of shock; for in shock, one's vision narrows and they are able to focus only on survival, such as a hypothermic person who can only think about getting to a warm place, and nothing else."
(Source: https://www.collinsdictionary.com)

I was quite convincing in my role as the *Rager;* or at least I thought I was. It was a grand facade that showed the world around me, and the truth within me, a distraction. As the rager, I was able to trade in my fear for reckless abandonment. There was something about this role as the rager I gravitated to; the energy I felt in it was addictive.

In 2015, I attended a workshop which featured Dr. Gabor Mate. In this Workshop he defined addiction as, "Any behaviour that gives a person temporary relief and pleasure, but also has negative consequences, and to which the individual returns to again and again."

I think the only reason I didn't become addicted to drugs or alcohol in my adolescence, was that my need for control was more intoxicating than any substance I had tried. Don't get me wrong, I'm not saying I'm not an addict, nor that I never abused drugs or alcohol. Quite the contrary actually. I tried a lot of drugs, and consumed a lot of alcohol. It took well into my adult life to recognize that my drug of choice, the one that first hooked me in, was *control.* In my teen years, 1 added raging. Unlike LSD or vodka, 1 decided when the high started and stopped. I felt like I finally had control over something, and I couldn't let it go.

Raging gave me some reprieve from the emotional pain I felt in fear. I had a trauma Superstore in my body; aisle upon aisle of

14

scary stories to pick from. I smashed windows, and got into fist fights with other girls. My rage afforded me another title on the 'streets' as the 'tough girl.'

The truth is that I hated this reputation. Even back then, I knew it wasn't me. I felt embarrassed and ashamed. I never told anybody how I really felt; I didn't believe anyone cared.

I wasn't willing to jeopardize the safety I found in control either. It was as if I was experiencing having choices for the first time in my life. I was continuing to abandon myself, but I was choosing when and how. I got lost for a while in this sea of rage. It was like I had shoved my essence into a burlap sack filled with bricks, and allowed rage to push me overboard. Having sunk to the bottom, what surrounded me there was not a beautiful blanket of coral, but instead, the weight of layers of shame.

Brene Brown defines shame in her book, *Dare to Lead*, as an "intensely painful feeling or experience of believing that we are flawed and therefore unworthy of love and belonging. It's an emotion that affects all of us and profoundly shapes the way we interact in the world."

> *Having drowned my own essence in shame, I left myself filling my mirror with a broken silhouette. As I grew older, I manifested that same fractured image.*

Brene Brown also speaks about shame in the episode "Brene on Shame and Accountability" in her podcast, *Unlocking Us with Brene Brown* series. She identifies the three things shame requires in order to grow: Secrecy, Silence and Judgment.

I certainly fulfilled those qualifications.

I never spoke to anybody about what happened to me behind closed doors. I kept secrets. I didn't talk back to the people who hurt me when I was a child; I kept silent.

What others might think if they knew what happened in my home worried me. Even what the people *in* my own home thought about what had happened to me, worried me. You see, I'd experienced sexual abuse as a child from people inside and outside of my family. I made no disclosure about the abuse until much later in my life. I'd held in the pain and trauma of these intimate assaults. Opening the chest of victimization I kept buried in the depths of my being welcomed a tidal wave of chaos within me. I felt painfully exposed. It was as if I had plunged myself naked in the icy waters of Antarctica.

No justice was served. No perpetrators were sent behind bars. There was just me. *I* felt like the caged one. Ironically, I feel I put myself on trial; only *I* was judge and jury. I found myself guilty. I penalized myself for being so fearful and weak.

I *could* insert an academic theory I researched, or some documented statistics detailing the short and long term impacts of childhood sexual abuse on victims. I *could,* but I don't have to. What I know to be true, is many of you reading this have experienced sexual abuse too.

Let me take this moment to tell you, "I'm sorry."

I'm so sorry that you had your trust ripped from your beautiful being, and I'm hopeful you are reading this today because *you are healing. I* am *the* expert in telling my life's experience. Being sexually abused as a child taught me that physical touch was scary and confusing. I learned to stay quiet and keep secrets. I always felt I had done something wrong. I believed I was bad, and that saying no was never an option. This lack of permission to set personal boundaries interrupted the connection with my internal messaging. Understanding the '*no*' feeling within me, is a natural child development skill that childhood sexual abuse robbed me of. Is it any wonder I would endure several surgeries and body breaks with this pre-existing disconnect from myself?

When my body said no, I didn't listen. Some of the basic emotional developmental milestones were blocked. My ability to trust myself and others with intimacy had been crippled by childhood sexual abuse. I developed a narrative of how to love and be loved that was given to me by eliminating boundary setting, and self care.

The line of communication from my brain to my body was riddled with shame, guilt, secrecy, silence, fear and confusion. These ingredients fueled my body for most of my life. I was in a cauldron of self sabotage, and completely unaware. I'd be stirred up every so often by a large spoon, hand-carved from my childhood trauma.

All of this begs the question: Is going back to your childhood always necessary? As a counsellor for over twenty years, I've met with a ton of resistance when making family of origin inquiries. Sometimes the parallels between childhood and present-day are obvious. Sometimes they're not. I've had to go back to my past, to better understand my present. I needed to make sense of the decisions I'd made, and sometimes still make.

It's like I was born as a full deck of cards, and life threw me across the floor. Now I'm playing 52-card pickup.

I chose to explain impact rather than share details of my sexual abuse. **If you're reading this, and can relate, I invite you to take a deep breath with me.** I've done, and will continue to do a lot of work releasing the shame of childhood sexual abuse. I release any responsibility for the thoughts, feelings and behaviours of my perpetrators. I retain full responsibility for healing my wounds. I'm also granting myself infinite time, and flexibility to heal. I see the breaks, surgeries and illness as the brilliance of my body crying out; craving self-love in an arena overflowing with trauma.

My body found a way when I was only 5 years old with my first set of stitches. An injury offered an opportunity to receive love. In the hospital a nurse's and doctor's only role is to heal the sick and hurt. My body had wisdom far beyond my years. My body figured out that I would not initiate self care. My body found a way to force self-care with each break, every stitch, and every surgery. I was loved and cared for in the hospital by complete strangers. I soaked up every ounce of love and care in those moments. Perhaps it was a painful price to pay to be loved? In some ways, it's not unlike sexual abuse. My body was used solely for pleasure and control by someone else. No respect was given to my body, and I mirrored that disrespect as I allowed my body to twist and break. But how brilliant is it that my young body figured out a way to sneak love in?!

I was starving for connection and belonging, but all I knew was what I had seen: connection was scary, painful and confusing. My body craved it nonetheless. My childhood experiences had taught me that the only alternative to being fearful, was becoming feared. So I dove into those icy waters of rage without consideration. I convinced many people throughout my teenage years that I was fearless; a Grammy-worthy performance that only provided more layers of shame.

Nevertheless, there were definitely moments of glory I felt in rage. And as I chronicle that rage through the expression of writing, I feel empowered in sharing that it felt good to rage back then. I knew that *how* I was expressing my anger wasn't *right,* but I felt a glorious freedom in opening the floodgates, and completely relinquishing control.

I remember a time I walked into an apartment and punched my fist through 3 windows. I remember the moments leading-up to the expression of my fury, feeling like I was going to explode. My boyfriend was in jail on assault charges, and I was being *watched* by his friends. I felt like I was living in a pressure cooker and the lid was about to blow off. The handful of stitches was a small price to pay for the utopian experience that blew the lid off the pot!

Shame, however, quickly filled my body when I let go of control this way. I worried about the people I hurt. As I write, I wonder if I was just caught in the crossfire of the *moments of glory* had by men who hurt me? Had they too felt bound by the need to control so intensely that rage was their only outlet? Perhaps the attacks were never personal? Perhaps I just happened to be walking the beaches when the tsunami hit.

I invite you to take a moment and consider a few things:
Women are conditioned to believe that punching is something

that mostly men do. When a man slams his fist on a desk, he's passionate. When a woman slams hers, she's too emotional. These *societal norms* force men and women into boxes of conformity. They encourage suppression of emotion. Men learn the only emotion they can express is anger; they feel shame or weakness expressing grief and fear. Women can fear their own anger, and shame themselves for expressing it.

"Don't cry like a girl," many men have been told. "Suck it up," or "I'll give you something to cry about!"

These are painful messages we have all heard at one time or another as children. These messages have shaped our beliefs about the role we allow our emotions to play in our lives. They impact how we develop relationships with each other, and first and foremost, the relationship we have with ourselves.

> *Before I continue, I invite you to take a moment to reflect on your own childhood messaging. What freedoms did you have to express emotion in your home? At school on the playground? Have you thought about how your childhood messaging has shaped your desire and/or abilities to connect with and express your emotions?*

Meanwhile, I set out into the dating world armed with beliefs and understandings of what an intimate relationship should look and feel like. At fifteen, I lived in a rooming house with my boyfriend. I couldn't wear short-sleeved shirts as they exposed the bruising imprints his merciless grip left on my arms. I wore a scar on my head from him smashing it off the corner of a wall in a club. I kept it hidden behind my bangs like a curtain of shame. I rarely fought back. I knew not to. What no one could see were the invisible scars inflicted upon my body like verbal lacerations.

This abuse further validated my belief, at that time, that the one with the power and control would always be the one who was safe. I learned something else from this experience in an abusive relationship: the one with the control also got what they wanted. At that time, I didn't understand the impact of the abuse I'd seen and experienced in my young life. I understand now that I was well equipped with the necessary tools to navigate a physically and verbally abusive relationship. Once again, remaining silent. Once again, keeping secrets.

Experiencing sexual abuse as a child afforded me layers of shame, and gifted me with another role as that of a rager. I lashed out on others, as I was more willing to stand in the spotlight of the hurt I was causing, then expose the darkness of shame I was feeling. I became addicted to control, and used the power I felt with it to hide pain that I felt was a weakness. Internal dialogue birthed in childhood sexual abuse is damaging to self and others. It can become the foundation for disconnected relationships with others, and for me added to the growing disconnect from myself. *Societal norms* are worth considering when exploring your relationship with each emotion, and how you choose to manage them.

"Vulnerability is not winning or losing; it's having the courage to show up and be seen when we have no control over the outcome."

BRENE BROWN

21

CHAPTER 3: THE BODY TALKS

I've come to understand that the emotional suppression I've endured over the years has created a significant physical impact on my body. Holding fear, anger, and grief in the body without providing regular outlets can be harmful.

 **Imagine your body as an electrical cord. If you tie several knots in the cord, the electrical current becomes weaker, even non-existent in places. Suppressed emotion does something similar in that it can manifest energetic knots or blockages in the body. These barriers impede the body's ability to function optimally.**

The body, however, does provide hints that the energy flow is weakening - if you're listening or aware. A symptom as simple as fatigue can be a gentle message from the body that an emotional blockage is present. Learning ways to release emotion renews the flow of energy throughout your body. This results in increased energy.

Here's something I do routinely that helps my flow of energy: It's a regular practice of mine to walk on the treadmill after work while watching *Grey's Anatomy*. Each episode is filled with opportunities to feel grief, fear and anger. You see, I don't always need to *talk* about my feelings. Watching a television series, especially while raising my heart rate, helps me release emotions I might be holding. The take home is that you can release emotions in a variety of ways, one of which could be indulging in the arts of any kind, including television shows.

Hundreds of events happen every day that evoke a multitude of emotional responses in our bodies.

HERE'S AN EXERCISE I'D LIKE TO SHARE

I invite you to think about yesterday. Can you recall how many times you felt sad, angry or scared? Perhaps you heard a song, watched the news, or inhaled an aroma that reminded you of someone. I'm not suggesting we have to cry every time we feel sad or hit a punching bag every time a car cuts us off. But I'm inviting you to welcome the awareness. I invite you to notice what you feel, and how much you feel throughout your day. Make a game of it! Challenge your friend or partner. Guess how many times you'll feel each of the three above mentioned emotions. Tally-up your totals at the end of the day.

You may be shocked to learn just how often you feel an emotion, yet hold it in. As we progress through this book, I'll be sharing examples of the physical impact on my body from years of suppressed emotion. As you move through reading what I've learned, I invite you to keep checking-in with yourself.

Think about physical injuries and illnesses you've experienced. Ask yourself what was happening in your life when you succumbed to those injuries and illnesses. How might your life be different if you're able to learn skills and techniques that worked for you to release emotion on a regular basis? I know my list of injuries would be much shorter had I known then what I know now about the impact holding-in emotions has had on my body.

For example, having gallstones at the early age of fourteen doesn't seem like a great mystery to me anymore. By that age, I'd developed a fear of anger. I hadn't learned yet that **anger, just like grief and fear, is a healthy emotion when expressed in a way that doesn't hurt anyone, anything, or oneself. I witnessed the wrath of both of my fathers, seeing and feeling the constellation of emotional scars they caused. I had concluded that anger was dangerous.** I would hold-in anger as long as possible. The results of holding in all of my anger? Like shaking a can of soda, blasts of rage that couldn't be contained! My body became a vault for shame, embarrassment and sorrow.

I held in the emotions that caused my family so much pain. Like holding your breath, eventually the body needs the oxygen. This self-destructive ripple effect of suppression, blasting then sucking it up again has exhausted my physical, and emotional body. Anger is held in the liver and gallbladder. Holding in anger caused more toxicity in my body, producing stones, I believe.

When I *blew my top*, I was left feeling deflated and empty. I was like a tire that had been over pumped, and expected to still endure the rough terrain. When I *blew up*, I felt ashamed and sad, but I held that in too.

My unexpressed *grief* further taxed my physical body, weighing it down with the fluids that needed releasing through tears.

Where did all of that fluid go? To my joints, I was already over-working in my role as an athlete. I was kind of a walking time bomb; and the countdown to blow seemed to be speeding up.

Had the medical professionals asked different questions, and valued the connections between emotional stress and physical symptoms back then, perhaps the removal of my gallbladder at the age of twenty-one could have been avoided.

My family doctor at the time was incredible, and spent time talking to me about my life. He was familiar with the family history and the abuse I had experienced and witnessed. He offered support with literature to read and tapes to listen to for Adult Children of Alcoholics. His support helped me feel seen. I even recall him sharing his own similar childhood story. The missing piece was addressing my unexpressed anger. What if the doctor asked me about my feelings, and if I was able to express them? It wasn't until I learned how to practice emotional releases that I stopped having pain related to gallstones.

I'll come back to this concept later, but I now know that unexpressed anger is held in the liver and the gallbladder. **Growing up in homes witnessing either unhealthy expressions of anger, or unexpressed anger meant that I was deprived of a safe outlet for my own emotions.** Both of my fathers used anger and rage to control, the result of which was the suppression and silencing of my mom. I know I felt anger, I just didn't express it. I believed that holding it in kept me safe. And without owning it, this led to a profoundly negative impact on my body.

When I feel anger surface in my body today, my response is very different. I now know that our bodies are incredible, and quite capable of enduring. I believe I'm proof of that. I think that the emotional impact of moving through life that way, however, creates unhealthy connections with self and others. This is why I **must constantly practice naming my feelings and learning how to release them or risk the consequences; the continued breakdown of my body, which leads to decreased mobility.**

As I've mentioned, I believe that **our bodies give us quiet messages (and sometimes not so quiet ones) when our internal reservoir of emotions are nearing the top. Energy is meant to come into the body and leave the body in a continuous flow. Those who study and practice *Shiatsu*, or *Reiki* for example, teach the necessity of moving energy through the body to avoid blockages.**

I've learned, and continue to practice listening and responding to the gentle messages my body offers when I'm feeling angry. I may notice a tenderness just under the right side, below my ribs. I might feel soreness in my jaw, or a dull ache in my shoulders that drifts along my shoulder blade. These three areas are right along the gallbladder *Meridian* which is associated with anger, as is the case with the liver. A meridian, in energy work, is best described as an energetic highway in the human body. The goal is to keep our highways clear, and avoid any blockages. Much like a car pile-up on the roadway can be caused by one driver slamming on their brakes, an unexpressed emotion may cause a blockage in your energy meridian creating a major traffic jam in your body.

27

After learning the signs and symptoms of each unexpressed emotion, I began to understand them as my body's way of waving at my mind and saying, "Heyyyy!, I'm feeling something, and I need some attention down here!"

Do you know what I mean? Have you got some familiar body cues that precede any of your emotions? What I've found is that ignoring the initial warnings created more painful consequences in the long run. The pain in my knee, when I ran, was my body's cry for some nurturing and attention. I didn't listen. This meant the next pop I heard wasn't that of a spritzer celebrating a victory after a game. No, it was my knee sending me to the orthopedic surgeon's office to book yet another surgical repair. It's like disregarding the small leak in your basement, until the next rainfall finds you stepping off the last stair into six inches of water.

Each emotion has a different list of physical symptoms. I've already mentioned a few of the signs and an illness connected to suppressed anger. At this point, I invite you to pay attention to what might come up for you as you continue reading. Holding your breath, difficulty regulating body temperature, frequent urination, low back ache, or headaches that feel like a vice grip around your skull are all symptoms of suppressed fear. And fear is held in the kidney and bladder meridians. Have you ever been just about to speak in front of a group of people and felt nervous? Suddenly, you're struck with a need to urinate. It's no wonder, isn't it?

Issues connected to your lungs or heart may be associated with suppressed grief or sadness. Sadness is held in the heart/lung and small intestine meridians. A feeling of heaviness in the chest or a cough that just won't go away, may be messages from your body that you're holding-in grief. I'll speak more to this later in the book, but invite you to start scanning your own bodies now. For me, this has been like learning a new language: body language. And I'm sharing this knowledge so that others may avoid the pitfalls that befell me or simply acquire the knowledge that might save years of suffering.

I imagine my body like a pond, with a feed and a runoff. The abuse in my home was the feed. The adults; mainly, both of my fathers, were exhibiting all of the anger, and made it unsafe for me to have mine, even to acknowledge that any anger existed. Don't get me wrong: mine was always there, but I held it in. Fear blocked the runoff of my pond. Now, allow me to ask you the following rhetorical question: What happens to water in a still pond? The stagnant water, like suppressed emotion in the body, breeds toxicity. This suppressed anger; this bottled-up toxicity, can cause physical illness like the gallstones I've already mentioned. Incredible, isn't it?

I jumped ahead because I'm excited to share this knowledge. I'm providing a pretext for what's to come as we explore how unexpressed emotion has such an incredible impact on our bodies.

In my own experience, I was always so fearful as a child. It took a lot of time and commitment, for me as an adult, to understand the extent of my unexpressed fear, and its painful impact on my self and my body. Because two of the signs and symptoms of unexpressed fear are confusion, as well as a difficulty taking-in information, it makes so much sense to me why learning and understanding my physical cues was so challenging.

However, I will need to take you back to the time and place I first met fear, so that we can explore the lead role it played in my life. It's going to be painful, but it's necessary. You'll see how my very first moments provided an encounter with fear that resonated for nearly the rest of my life. And then you'll see how forty years later, I was finally able to figure out that, all along, I'd been working on a gigantic puzzle; a puzzle that now makes sense to me. This initial greeting with fear severed the embrace between my body and my essence with the fury of a lightning bolt. I now understand why the reunification of my physical and emotional self over forty years later proved to be equally shocking.

Our bodies speak to us all the time, and I believe the better we can understand the messages, the more quickly and accurately we can respond with the care that is required. Be kind to you, as you consider what you have experienced in your own body as you continue reading.

"She was powerful, not because she wasn't scared but because she went on strongly, despite the fear."

ATTICUS

CHAPTER 4: THE ROBOT

Dreams have played an important role in my life. In addition to my body trying to get me to notice it, I'm certain that my mind used times of rest to whisper wisdom in my ears by way of stories and imagery.

My first memories of being afraid as a child appear like still photos in my mind. I recall a recurring dream I had in my early years of kneeling in the grass beside the apartment building of the 5th address we lived in during the first five years of my life.

By that time, my mom had left my biological father. We packed-up and moved-on each time my father found our address. If we were a circus family, these multiple moves would have been expected. My Dad did seem like the Ringmaster, however. Each time he cracked his whip, we responded obediently like animals. We would jump through any hoop, and do somersaults if it kept us safe. My mom juggled work, court, and caring for us tirelessly, just to keep us safe. I don't know how she survived. I only remember pieces; perhaps that's how *I* survived. I remember doors getting smashed in, and my Gramps sitting by his window, shotgun on his lap, while my father drove by the house with his headlights off.

I used to dream that I had two friends who were miniature people I could hold in the palm of my hand. I would keep them close to me, allowing them the freedom to climb weeds, which for them were like large willow trees. A gust of wind would blow, nearly throwing my two little friends off of their branches. I would swiftly scoop them up into the safety of my hands. And just before I would run away, I would glance back to see a larger than life red-eyed robot charging towards us.

The dream was always the same. I was alone with my little ones, and the scary robot was going to get us. It's so interesting to me that in my dream, the instinct was to protect my *little ones;* yet in life, I'd made conscious decisions to run directly towards the scary robot. I would continue to make these *seemingly* self-destructive decisions for most of my life. I was trying to escape the pain of having no control and feeling abandoned.

Interestingly, I'm fascinated by how children adapt to their environment and get their needs met. Have you ever heard stories about yourself as a child, or watched a child in the throes of a temper tantrum and thought, "How amazingly brilliant?!" A screaming fit on the floor in the middle of a grocery store is a surefire way to get the attention of the adults in your life! It's *also* a powerful method of *cutting to the chase,* and releasing the feelings! Imagine the reaction you or I might get if we let out a high pitched scream at the movies during a scary scene? What if you were watching a work presentation and a story made us sad, and we started to wail? We have created *socially acceptable* ways to release feelings. The huge roller coasters, or extreme sports where a scream would be viewed as *acceptable* in society. What might it be like if we adapted some of our childhood wisdom? *Owning* our feelings AND expressing them when they arise, rather than sucking them up? How might our life be different?!

My childhood was scary. We moved six times in the first eight years of my life. It's no wonder I developed a love for jogging. After all, my mom taught me that running was a necessary part of survival; run or be hurt, or run and still get hurt. I remember feeling fear and hearing words like "gun" and "hide," but my first clear images are that of clumps of hair and blood. I remember muffled sounds like the wind the robot made in my dream, only there were no little ones for me to protect and run away with. I guess I was the little one this time. My dad had broken down another door and violently assaulted my mom's friend.

My biological father wasn't a very tall man, but he had the presence of a black bear. Seemingly harmless from a distance; a black bear, under attack, can bend a car door in half. My father's hands were like thick paws and always showcased two large gold rings. He was an athlete in his younger years and played defense on his soccer team; though my mom said he was a good athlete, but a really poor sport. The year he died he was 64, and yet his jet black hair had not one gray strand. His eyes were dark; they projected a distrust for others, and were forever surveilling a room. A police officer for years, I wonder if his need to control worsened with the trauma he experienced on the job. My mom said I have his broad shoulders, and I think I have my father's lips, though his mouth was used to interrogate rather than to connect. When I began to learn about energy work later in life, and where we hold sadness in the body, it made sense to me that my Dad died of a heart attack. I imagine he found sadness and grief too vulnerable, and not a state of emotion in which he opted to experience and express.

The day my father attacked my mother's friend, the police came. And I believe this is when I exited my body. I remember moving down the hall towards the room where the violence had occurred. The voices are muffled in my memory, perhaps drowned out by my own racing heart beat. Images and sounds came and went from my eyes and ears; then silence.

What happened next, in this fifth address I called home as a child, I don't remember. It's still disturbing to me when my mom retells my actions:

I begged to go with my father.

I begged to go with the perpetrator of such extreme violence; the man who broke into our home, committed a brutal assault, left clumps of hair on the floor, and called me his daughter.

That's who I wanted to go with.

I looked at my sister and mom on one side of the room, huddled in a corner crying. I saw my dad, with the shoulders of a linebacker now filling the space where our front door used to hang. He was calm and in control despite the blood on his hands. The officer stood with my dad, and appeared to be engaged in casual chatter.

At five years old, I must have done a quick survey of the room and made the only logical decision: Perhaps I believed if I chose him, he wouldn't hurt me? A kind of, *keep your enemies closer*, survival strategy. I don't know for certain. I just know that I did what I believed I should have done at that moment.

I was terrified, confused, and wishing I was somewhere else. I wanted to be somewhere safe; somewhere I had control. I can only assume that the terror was more than my young self could bear. I believe that in the midst of this trauma, I was so overcome with fear that I made a decision. Standing in the living room in the presence of my father; the police, the yelling, my mother, the tears, and my big sister; I ran towards fear.

I could no longer bear having such a lack of control, so I ran into the arms of the man who had it.

I hid my fear and my pain; denying they even existed. I now know this decision was a pivotal moment in my life. Staying close to the person in control was safer than cowering in the corner in the shadow of his fist. Holding emotions like fear in the body meant reducing the risk of exposing vulnerability. Denying the need for nurturing or praise meant removing the vulnerability that felt like a target on my back. This decision would shape my relationships with friends, with family, with *intimacy* and ultimately with myself.

Looking back, I can't help but wonder if this pivotal moment where I slammed the door shut to myself, had something greater than me crack a door open? Did my complete abandonment of myself for survival find me, like the *Footprints* poem illustrates, picked up by spirit and carried?

I continued to experience this robot dream well into my adult life. I'd always assumed the robot represented my biological father. Seems logical; he was big, scary, and he had power over people. But what if I was wrong? What if he wasn't the robot in my dream? What if *I* was the robot?!

The robot in my dream scared me, but he wasn't actually scary to look at. He was kind of cartoon-like. He had a square head, a rectangular body, and two spinning antennas on top of his head. His legs and arms were like gray tubular accordions. Doesn't sound very scary, right? Yet in my dream, the *little* people I was protecting were terrified. Perhaps the little people represented *my own* vulnerability; specifically my grief and anger? What if *I* was represented by the scary metal shell, held together by bolts and screws, like the plates and pins from multiple orthopedic surgeries? An empty metal robot designed to host a multitude of roles. A robot that kept my *essence* running and hiding; holding in my grief and anger. The robot remained charged by fear and control. Might I have been holding-in my own vulnerability within a metal shell, behind bars welded together with fear?

I identified the pivotal moment in my life when I unconsciously set aside my needs and wants, and chose the safety of my abusive father. I believe I traded in my *essence,* for the safety I witnessed in what my young self perceived to be, control. Needing control drove my decisions beginning at the age of five. My dream tells the tale of my first childhood trauma, and the imagery is powerful, and has afforded me years of processing and pulling wisdom from it.

"Never let your fear decide your future."

UNKNOWN

CHAPTER 5: IRISH EYES

As my childhood story unfolded, I developed roles to keep myself safe. All I had to do was figure out what role best suited the environment in which I was placed. Each role would act like a suit of armour or an identity that I controlled. I became a performer of sorts, but was also terrified of the spotlight. I could control what others might see or expect from me. If I accurately depicted the role and met the needs of the individuals in my environment, I felt chosen.

Losing and denying pieces of myself, my values, my dignity, my emotions, and my needs was a price I paid to be chosen. My dad gained control using fear. I gained control by denying it. If I'm not scared, I won't be hurt. I could step into a role, then jump into a scary scenario to prove I was fearless. I worked hard to convince the world I was never scared; my roles hid my vulnerability. And yet, my body kept trying to 'oust' me by breaking. This is a huge part of my story that I will share. Yet despite how hard I pushed myself, it was the injuries, the surgeries, and the illnesses that finally stopped me from playing. My body had become a broken home, that would *eventually* no longer house my pain.

To know is to be familiar; in familiarity there's a sense of control. If I had control, I could be safe. This false sense of safety set me on a self-destructive path. I took the scary story I was given by the adults in my life and made it my own. I took control of my fear and my pain by deciding when and how I would feel it; yet another piece of irony that I failed to see until many years later. And since I was the interpreter of the story I'd been given, I was also capable of healing my pain and creating my own story. Much like a turtle retreats into its shell for safety, l stepped into my story; an environment l knew well.

What a resilient and brilliant animal the turtle is. With a powerful protective shell, a safe space within which to retreat, and movement that's cautiously intentional, the turtle is an animal I greatly admire. I have turtle pieces and images spread throughout my home; reminders to my *younger self* that I am healing. I may be working at a turtle's pace, but I'm growing an increased fascination and love of my very own story.

I've heard the comparison that healing is like peeling away at an onion: Each layer is difficult to peel back, and sometimes what's revealed makes the eyes water! Like the turtle, I kept hidden inside my shell when I was scared. The soft parts of me that felt most vulnerable; my fear, my voice, were tucked away safely out of sight. You might say that, even in the womb, I was turtling, well aware of the trauma my mother was incurring, only waiting to come out in order to create my own shell.

Our next home looked very different from the first five in which I lived. It came with a front door that was never kicked-in. This new home had no elevator, and the back door led to a yard instead of a parking lot. We were next to a huge park with swings, slides, and a baseball diamond instead of a row of self-serve car washes. Incidentally, the carwash was the scene of my first ever fall; resulting in my first trip to the emergency room.

My mom always said I was an accident waiting to happen. I wonder if she had any idea how many trips to the hospital were in my future? Was this the first of my cries for help breaks? Did the cry come from me, or my body?

I had my own bike, and a neighborhood block that filled two of my pillow cases with candy every Halloween. I had my very own room, and my sister was especially excited about that! Sharing a room in our apartment was no fun for my big sister. She did find amusement when dividing our room with tape, and insisting I couldn't move because the door was on her side of the line!

I felt chosen for the first time in this home. We were introduced to two amazing humans we got to call Nana and Grandad. My Nana had a long mane of gray hair she kept neatly in a clip; she later replaced the length with a perfect head of loose curls. Her eyes were a light blue that sparkled like the sun off a glacier. Nana made scones with raisins, and drank tea with me. I filled my cup with piles of sugar, and she never stopped me from adding more. She spoke with an accent even sweeter than my tea; her words moved softly from her tiny lips. She had a smile that demanded nothing. She wrapped me in her homemade apron when we visited, and let me play waitress, both serving and consuming traditional Irish treats. She taught me how to play UNO, and always treated me like the star of her favourite show.

Somehow she knew all about inclusivity and acceptance long before those terms and practices became mainstream. She was a devout Christian; her bible overflowed with her writings and slips of scripture-filled papers. I imagine she found strength in her faith, having grown up in Northern Ireland and being married to a husband in the Royal Air Force. She practiced the word of God as she interpreted it, but she didn't preach. She was the epitome of humility and selflessness. My step dad gave me her bible recently; such a priceless gift. I found a poem she had written in the back that truly describes her essence:

Others may be stained glass of rainbow hue.
I would be a window pane for the sun to shine through.
A clear glass, a clean glass is what I would be;
Unconcerned with temperament and personality.
I would have the sun shine through me, so my friends would
say, Not, "What a lovely pane," but, "What a lovely day."

KATHRINE GUINN

I've read this poem many times since finding it. My Nana passed away when I was a young teenager, yet this poem makes me feel so connected to her today. I wonder if there were other emotions my Nana kept cocooned behind her selfless smile. I wonder if in this poem she is cleverly and safely exposing how she hid her other emotions. I can't help but marvel at the timing of this poem showing up for me! It feels too intentional to be a coincidence.

She shone a spotlight on others, she listened, and she applauded. She never stepped on stage herself, yet she was so deserving of having *her* voice heard. If she were here today, I have no doubt she would say the very same about me. I resonate with my perception of this poem, and the role my Nana held in her life as I saw her.

She died from cancer in her stomach and pancreas; the organs associated with nurturing, or lack of it. I wonder how different her life might have been had she been able to express all of her feelings she held inside her body? Her poem further validates the current journey I'm on that I'll speak about later; birthing from that cocoon of suppression, and releasing all of my emotions. I'm truly loving this part of sharing my story that has me giving voice and center stage to the infinite wisdom of my grandparents.

Along with her only son, my Nana placed her husband, my Grandad, on a podium. He did not own a bible like my Nana, and he didn't practice or preach the word of God. He was, however, a poet, and documented many of his literary creations. He had a thick mass of wintery white hair that he kept neatly shaped with Brylcreem. His eyes were a brilliant blue that actually twinkled when he smiled. His cheeks were full and his nose told tales of the years of alcohol use.

My Grandad had a unique spirit that overflowed when he consumed too many of his *own* spirits. He loved his beer and his cigarettes, and I spent many nights listening to his favourite war stories. I was fascinated by his storytelling, and how his cigarette ash would cling to the end of the filter like a pool noodle. He told stories of receiving a bullet to his body through an aircraft while in flight. He was outrun by a fella with an aluminum leg when a bomb landed just beside the building they were playing cards in! He shared these experiences with me as if reading from a book of fictional war tales. His face was as animated as his arms, and his laugh was so contagious.

He used alcohol and humour to numb the impact of his trauma. My Grandad suffered two heart attacks, the second of which took his life.

Perhaps his heart could no longer hold his unexpressed grief?

He endured so many losses; loss of innocence, loss of connection to his wife and son, and perhaps even to himself. I wonder if using humour to release emotion wasn't enough to relieve the burden of emotional trauma that consumed my Grandad's body?

Although my Nana and Grandad were not my biological grandparents, they treated me like they chose me. There was an obvious tension between my grandad and his only son, who I will soon introduce as my stepfather. I wonder how capable my Grandad was of loving and connecting with his son in a body so riddled with trauma? With the only counseling or therapy my granddad received being the contents of a beer bottle, what tools did he have after the war to heal? It seems obvious why my stepfather needed to have control. Perhaps just as reading my Nana's poem has me feeling so connected to her decades after her death, telling the story about the lack of father/son bond unveils an experiential parallel I can now see so clearly between my stepfather and me. Maybe my Nana wasn't able to put my stepfather on stage like she did me. She was, after all, busy supporting a husband abusing alcohol and suppressing trauma. I'm sure she gave him all she could. What I know from experience is we develop a perception of ourselves based on how *we see* our parents love each other, AND from the way in which they love *themselves*.

The realization of this connection between my stepfather and me is very healing. Maybe he grew up with a ton of unexpressed fear too? It also has me wondering if my Grandad's smile was a mask for *his* grief? In my training of *Psychodramatic Bodywork*®,

I've learned that grief and sadness are held in the heart and lungs. What if he was taught how to identify feelings, and how to ask for support, expressing them throughout his life? I wonder if he had this knowledge, how different my stepfather's relationship with emotions might have been. Anger is just one emotion. How different their connection might have been if fear and sadness were openly expressed and accepted in each other. Perhaps the one way he found to express his love for his son, my stepfather, was in his writing.

> *"My Son - and Me"*
> *Blue-eyed and bright*
> *Like a ray of light*
> *There never was one better*
> *A bundle of love*
> *From God above*
> *His daddy to the letter*

ANDREW GUINN

This is just a piece of one of my Grandad's poems. It was about twelve or so verses long. Each verse ended with, "His daddy to the letter." My Granddad is no longer with us, so like my Nana's poem, I'm left with just my own perspective. This lengthy poem reads much like the *Cat's in the Cradle*, by Harry Chapin. Perhaps my Grandad wrote this while he was stationed somewhere. Maybe he wrote it after my stepfather had grown, while he sat reflecting on the years he spent away from home not raising his son. I wonder If my Grandad hoped his words would one day be read by his son, and the sentiments would support him in healing, having grown up with an absent father.

I learned to trade in my essence for control at the age of five, and to continue self abandonment to be chosen throughout my childhood. I learned very young that love was conditional. I did, however, experience unconditional love from my Grandparents. I was unaffected by the wounding *they* had experienced in their lives. They were brilliant at hiding their trauma from me when I was a child, for the most part. As an adult I'm able to read between the lines of the stories they told, and the silence they kept. I hold more empathy for, and awareness of their pain, and compassion for their coping mechanisms today.

"We must reject not only the stereotypes that others hold of us, but also the stereotypes that we hold of ourselves."

SHIRLEY CHISHOLM

CHAPTER 6: TONY

As I shared earlier, Nana and Grandad came with a new home, complete with a front door that had never been kicked-in. The new home also came with a big brother. He flew in from Wisconsin to live with his Dad, my new stepfather, every summer. He appeared about 7 feet tall to me back then, though I grew to realize he was actually just 5'10".

 I went with my stepdad to pick him up from the airport. The days building up to his arrival felt like an eternity. I think most kids get excited about summer vacation, but it meant so much more for me. They were the most exciting months of the year! To this day, I live for the summer months. I often get butterflies when I look out and see the sun shining brightly. I just have to get out and feel the sun on my face! Remembering how I counted down the days to see Tony, makes me wonder if my *summer butterflies* adjusted to their migration pattern from my childhood? I would stand, gripping the railing at the arrival gate. My eyes, wide with anticipation, could not be peeled away from the doors. It took everything in me to control myself from jumping up and down. It was like waiting for the gate to open to board your favourite ride at the amusement park.

Finally! The doors slid open revealing my tall, dark and handsome, blue-eyed brother. He appeared like a movie star to me walking the red carpet toward us. Those first few years I could only conjure up a giggle from my burning red face when he would hand me his duffle bag filled with deflated balls and a tennis racket. I received it like it was the holy grail. I'd walk through the airport carrying that bag as proud as a peacock. His walk was more like a stroll, and was as unique as his Racine accent. His thick wavy hair perfectly matched his charismatic smile that captivated any audience. I set him up on a pedestal the moment I met him. I had a big brother! He let me play tennis with him from the *outside* of the court. He said he and his friends needed to hit the ball *on* the court, and my important role was to retrieve stray balls. I was so excited to have such an important role! Again, I felt chosen.

Tony always made time to sing *Danny Boy* for me, especially the night before he went back to Wisconsin. I sat at his feet and wished the song would never end. To this day, whenever I hear that song, I can picture my young self wrapped in my brother's love and safety. Have you ever noticed how powerfully a song can evoke physical sensations in your body? Or how a song can wring the tears right out from your chest like a sponge? How hearing the words of a chorus can flip your stomach inside out? I hated when he left. His voice and the strumming of his guitar wrapped me in warmth like my Nana's apron. My chest would ache while he sang.

I now understand that dreadful feeling in my chest, in my heart and lungs where unexpressed sadness is held. I was grieving my brother's departure. I didn't cry back then. That would be *weak*. The weak are targeted and hurt; I wanted to be chosen, not hurt.

As a young person, I *decided* that being sad and scared was weak. I saw my mom being scared and sad while being controlled and abused. Seems like a logical conclusion for a child, doesn't it? The sad and the scared get hurt. I think this was a rather brilliant deduction I'd made at such a young age. If I could take control of my sadness and fear by denying them, it was more likely that I'd be safe. With anger being an emotion the adult men in my life were having so much of, I held that in too. Having safely filed away sadness, fear, and anger, I hoped it would create space for joy. At the very least, faking an expression of joy was easy. Thus began the process of dressing my life like the facade of a home. While my body housed the trauma, my home was staged, quite precariously, with a smile.

Even letting my own brother know that I was sad or scared didn't feel like an option for me, growing up. I needed to have control over being chosen. My need to control blocked my ability to trust anyone, including myself. I'd have to say goodbye to Tony, and I wouldn't see or hear from him again until the following summer break. I worried he would forget about me while he was gone; or worse, maybe he wouldn't come back at all. If I told him how intensely I would miss him, I would appear needy. That wouldn't be good either. After all, I had a toxic nurtured belief that having emotional needs only leads to pain and abandonment. But I did imagine how I could fit in his suitcase, flattened with his deflated soccer ball and tennis racket! Many years later he would confess that he too wished he could have snuck my sis and I on the plane back to Wisconsin with him.

Since deciding to open the *vault of family stories* with my brother, every conversation between us has been rich with emotions and more insights about ourselves . As I hung off his leg from the time he landed every summer, my admiration is no surprise to Tony; he knows it. But it's not easy for him to claim. He too grew-up feeling he wasn't enough. He's now a well known Head Coach of a men's soccer team in America and has won multiple awards for his coaching abilities. He's a big deal in the American college coaching world. He remains a big deal in my world too. As I continue to unveil myself, the pedestal that I once created for Tony has been transformed into a two-seater bench, on which I sit with my beloved stepbrother.

Tony recently texted me: "You're just awesome. Admit it, we all know it."

I see the brilliance and the resolve in our shared drive to succeed. I also recognize the parallels in our respective journeys of physical injury and illness. We can spend hours talking about our sports injuries; like old war veterans sharing battle scars. I will forever listen to the wisdom my big brother has to offer. I also embrace the space I create for Tony to learn from my process.

In fact, it was my brother who first introduced me to sports and competition. The first time I felt the lactic burn, I was hooked. I had secured a role I could safely hide in. I could run miles, play soccer, sweat my butt off wearing only a smile as an athlete. I was also learning that the more roles I created, the more opportunities this would provide to feel chosen. I often pushed my body far beyond my comfort level. I was forever driven to beat my greatest opponent: myself. When I felt pain in sport, I told myself to push harder. "No pain, no gain," was a commonly quoted phrase in the 80s, and I took it to heart.

I now recognize that the drive to push my body beyond comfortable limits was a means of exercising control. I had finally found a way to control my own pain. Instead of living in fear and suspense, waiting to be scared and hurt, I took charge of the pain and fear. I got to control my pain by inflicting it; and I got to control my fear by denying it. Plus, there was the nurturing from nurses, a welcome byproduct of my many injuries. In the hospital, the nurses wrapped me in warm flannel sheets. It was as if I was being swaddled like an infant. Incapacitated by pain medication and a surgical repair that required stillness, I could justify *doing nothing* to myself without guilt. *"Idle hands are the devil's work."* Keeping busy meant being productive and having value. "Sitting still was for the lazy." This is what I *used* to think.

As an athlete, I couldn't be accused of laziness. The expectations of self and others were clear to me too. In this role, I felt I had control. I perceived that with control came safety. When I played soccer, I knew what my teammates expected of me. There was no place for fear and tears on a soccer pitch. I could be in a role and experience connection with minimal risk of exposing the vulnerability of my feelings. I could control them. The only feelings expressed in a game were anger and joy. In my role as an athlete, I had no issue with anger. I could allow some of my fear to sneak out in big blasts of rage on the field where it was accepted. I now see that I had no clue, back then, of what I was doing. My behaviour afforded me the label of "poor sport" by my mother. But I preferred that to "weakling." The weak get hurt by others. I'd made the unconscious decision at a young age that I would control how and when I was hurt. This meant the perpetrator of my pain was often *myself.*

I want to pause at this moment. I need to highlight just how powerfully I injected my childhood trauma into my growing self. When I made the unconscious decision to deny my fear and sadness, it was as if I then replaced them with syringes filled with control. Anytime a feeling came-up that resonated with past trauma, I gave myself a little shot. Each injection wasn't a cure. On the contrary, I treated fear and grief like a virus. The main symptom was vulnerability. Denying fear and sadness kept me safe when I felt unsafe, which I told myself was all the time. Holding-in these emotions when I was safe was keeping me in a perpetual loop of trauma. Like the definition of insanity, I was repeatedly injecting past coping strategies into the present, unaware of the changes in my environment.

I created the role of athlete at a young age to earn the acceptance and love of my stepbrother. I believed that athletes were strong and confident. I also believed that crying was a sign of weakness, and athletes didn't cry. I wanted to be what I perceived my brother to be, in order to be good enough for him. What I've come to learn is that my athleticism afforded me a physical outlet, but enduring pain by holding in emotion kept me from connecting with myself, and my brother. The harder I pushed myself, the more I pushed my brother, and others away.

"The greatest gift you can give someone, is your time."

UNKNOWN

CHAPTER 7: FEAR

My body's been speaking to me my whole life. Thankfully, in my forties, I began to learn my *own* language; the language my body had been trying to convey. Most of my life's been spent using the gifts my faculties afforded me, including intuition, to learn and mirror the language of others. Though becoming affluent in recognizing and meeting the needs of others gave me meaning and purpose, denying my own needs came at a painful price to my body, mind and Spirit. I had numerous falls and breaks requiring multiple trips to the emergency room by the time I reached eighth grade. Were my falls and breaks due to my clumsiness, or proof of my degree of fear and disconnect from myself? Was I crying out for attention, or for justified traumas to release my tears? Did I begin to develop gallstones at fourteen because of genetics, or had my body overfilled with unexpressed anger, leaving it no choice but to retaliate with illness? Was I unconsciously creating opportunities to feel and release vulnerability, safely?

My list of injuries is exhaustingly long. I have often found myself wishing I was a gifted poet or songwriter. I would have you tapping your feet to the beat as I sang my list of body woes with an artistic flair. Perhaps you can imagine me as an archaeologist, like Indiana Jones. My body, like that of a treasure map, would have several Xs, each of them marking the spot of a previous injury, leading to a valuable clue. In order to fully understand each clue as I navigate you through this map of injuries, I would need to include a detailed legend with the map. **The legend would offer a detailed list of the signs and symptoms of unexpressed fear.** This list would offer insights, and ultimately reveal the treasure; *my* Holy Grail, if you will; an awareness and understanding of my *own* body language. It's this very list that has helped me listen to my body, and become my *own interpreter*. It's as if I've been able to tear the tape off the mouth of my body, and in doing so, become an attentive audience.

Possible signs and symptoms of unexpressed FEAR (As created by Susan Aaron, listed in her Workshop Manual, and copywritten):

- A general lack of vitality
- When frightened, a feeling of cold. Potential shivering
- Frequent urination
- Bladder infections, kidney stones and yeast infections
- Difficulty hearing, excess wax buildup in the ears, ear infections or itchy ears.
- Rotting, weak, or falling out teeth
- Hair that suddenly falls out, turns gray- white or changes texture
- Difficulty in sleeping due to night urination, night sweats and nightmares.
- Breath irregularities that can include hyperventilation, rapid breathing and holding our breath
- Feeling ungrounded
- Being frozen stiff, paralyzed, or unable to move or speak
- Acute or chronic low back ache or pain

- Eyes that often appear either closed or completely open wide and glazed over.
- Sweaty, cold palms
- Daydreaming, splitting off, spacing out and dissociating
- Suddenly feeling extremely sleepy and falling asleep
- Phobias
- Specific headaches that start at the base of the neck and come upward to feel like a cap on the top of the head
- Heart palpitations and panic attacks

Notice how many items on the list are very common symptoms that people learn to live with. Many don't even realize that they have a possible connection to unexpressed fear. How might one confirm their suspicions? There are many fear releasing exercises that support the body by moving this fearful energy out. Screaming into a pillow, or shaking the arms and legs are two techniques you can do on your own to release some fear. Though these two actions sound easy, they are best done with an individual *trained* in release work.

Learning and understanding the signs and symptoms of unexpressed fear helped me understand and welcome compassion for my lengthy list of falls in the first twelve years of my life. I believe I was *ungrounded*, and often dissociated as a child, filled with unexpressed fear.

One of my greatest epiphanies was recognizing the titanium container I *assumed* my body to be; which represented a response to my fearful childhood traumas. Fear dictated the need for an unbreachable being. In that miscontrived manner, the shell of my being would no longer be broken. I laid the foundation of my container with fear, like that of concrete for a home. My teenage years would find me piling-on anger and grief, like bricks and mortar. Ironically, unmentioned, yet so unconsciously protected, lived my heart.

Recognizing the symptoms has lifted a layer of self judgment. I was never clumsy. I wasn't weak. I wasn't even uncoordinated, nor was I lacking the desire to love and be loved, I was *avoiding* the risks of feeling more pain. There was *nothing wrong* with me. I was *simply* scared.

As I walk you through the following list of incidents, I invite *you* to think back. Have you experienced many falls or accidents in your life? Have you ever thought about what was happening in your life around the time of those events?

My first traumatic fall was before my second birthday. I rolled down a full flight of stairs. My mom, sister and I were living in our first home with my biological father. Crisis and chaos were in full bloom in that first home. Was this fall an accident? Or was I already developing my *signature moves* to receive nurturing?

At the age of five, while running, I fell in a self-serve car wash. My friend was pretending to spray me with a hose. I remember hearing the echo of my own laughter rebounding off the metal walls. My laughing came to a thunderous halt when my head hit the concrete. My mom's face, when she opened the door, was confusing to me. Perhaps she wondered why the car wash attendant was holding me? She must have needed a moment to digest her five-year-old standing there, blood seeping through the oil stained cloth? A trip to the hospital and 10 stitches across my forehead followed.

In grade five, I fell and broke a couple of fingers playing football. I remember this one well. The two boys were acting pretty *sour* that I could outrun them, so they planned to trip me on the last play! My sister greeted me when I got home. With wide eyes, and action before thought, she grabbed the arm of my newly broken hand and yelled, "Oh my god, what happened??" I like to think that I provided the inspiration for her current nursing career. Next scene, I recall waiting to have my fingers set and a cast fitted. My mom, the teacher, handed me a pen and paper. I was right handed, and about to have my writing hand casted. My mom insisted I begin practicing with my left hand. "We don't want to see your school work suffer." She said. I know she meant well. Looking back, I wonder how that experience might have been for me had I just been held and able to cry? I wonder if my *mom* was ever scooped-up and held in *her* tears when she was a little girl?

In grade six, I had my tonsils and adenoids removed. On my first recess back to school, I stepped out through the school doors only to meet a rubber ball, right in the nose! A trip back to emerge followed. The packing was placed back in my nose, and a note was sent with me to my teacher restricting outdoor recess for a week!

In grade seven, practicing for the finals in track and field, I missed the mat completely in high jump, landing on the concrete. That resulted in an ambulance ride to emerge, and luckily just a bruised tailbone. Later in grade seven, I fell off the back of a friend's bike. It's a good thing I learned to write with my left hand, my mom said! Another trip to emerge, and another soft cast on my right hand. I think the office should have just left a designated chair in the office just for me every time I broke!

Grade eight was pretty quiet, with just a fainting spell in the kitchen. My mom came running out saying, "I heard a loud bang! What was that?!" I told her it was just me banging the cupboards. But I had been preparing for the public speaking finals. They were to be held in the gym that day, and I would be first to present. I woke up on the floor of the kitchen with the glass of water I had poured on my face! I didn't want to tell my mom because I didn't want to miss giving my speech. I remember feeling certain I'd be a winner!

Looking back, I can see that I gave my mom plenty of material to sew together my label of, *The accident waiting to happen!* My final injury in public school is forever archived in my grade 8 graduation photo. It was a scar across my forehead from a basketball game; a foreshadowing of the new list of injuries I would soon be experiencing.

There's no doubt sport has been, and continues to be an incredible *outlet* in my life. Using sport and athleticism was the safest way to release unexpressed emotions. I continue to use fitness as a healthy physical and emotional release. The difference today is that I push my body. In the past, I did not *push* my body, l punished it. I ignored the need for rest. If I felt tired or in pain, I told myself I was weak and needed to train harder. Where did such harmful self-talk come from? I would do a lot of personal work in my twenties and thirties. It was, however, in my 40th year that I had an experience that changed my inner dialogue forever.

In my teen years, the signs and symptoms of unexpressed fear persisted, but I was showing-up with a new list of injuries. I began adding something new to my growing medical files too:

illness. Scheduled visits to the hospital became more frequent than my spontaneous emergency room arrivals.

Having left home before fifteen, and fully immersed in a physically abusive relationship, the unexpressed fear in my body was joined by anger. I believe I'd already become well-read in holding-in anger. My titanium shell was impenetrable. As a child, the men in my life taught me that anger and violence were *one*. The abusive relationship I was in mimicked a familiar environment. He chose me, and the relationship became a mirror image of the only type of relationship I knew. He got what he wanted, when he wanted it. My needs didn't matter; and if they did, I had no idea what they were back then to share with someone. I was the *tackle dummy* for his pain. Before I knew it, my forehead became a billboard, advertising his anger with 12 stitches. That incident dispelled the myth that breaking up in a public place would ensure safety. There would be countless bruises in the shape of handprints on the back of my arms, my head going through walls, charges laid and dropped, and several *walks of shame* down my high school hallway wearing a black eye before the chapter was done. I'd even have my favourite law teacher slip a note into my pocket that read, "Do me a professional and personal favour, and go see these people." The address of the local women's abuse shelter was written in bold print across the card. I read the card and slipped it swiftly back in my pocket. I didn't want anyone to see. I didn't want anybody to know. I was ashamed. And my peers always assumed I was in a fight. Looking back, it validates the *grand facade* I'd so masterfully created. My secrets needed to remain locked up inside.

Of course I had no idea the counsellor I would see would be my colleague one day. I'd be joining her and many others in the fight for violence against women, years later! I felt embarrassed, and exposed… and a wee bit cared for. The latter feeling was weird: "How has Mr. Bows seen through all of this?" I asked myself. "Holy shit! What does the other girl look like?" were the comments in the hallways from my peers. I wondered if my facade was crumbling. Had there been a breach of my titanium hull? I will share, however, that the relationship did finally end. Full disclosure; I didn't end it. He did. He chose when it started, and when he would replace me with another girl to be his tackle dummy.

Unlike him, I rarely sourced out a human tackle dummy for my anger. I just used myself. The few bombs of rage I did drop, however, sucked me deep into the vacuum of shame and guilt. Like holding in fear, **unexpressed anger has associated signs and symptoms. Anger is held in the gallbladder and liver.** I was being tested and treated for a stomach ulcer in grade nine which was, by twenty-one, as I mentioned before, diagnosed as gallstones. Even after my gallbladder removal, I continued to experience gallstones that irritated the interior of my bile duct. I had three additional procedures; the final one resulting in having my bile duct being snipped at age thirty-eight. The surgeon said I had so much scar tissue that the tiniest of stones couldn't glide through the duct without causing moderate to severe spasms. It was as if my body had reached its limit of unexpressed anger. The tiniest hint of resentment was enough to send my body into painful spasms. Back then, no connection was made between my relationship with anger and my gallstones. Western medicine was accurate in my physical diagnosis and treatment. However, my emotional body was never examined for questions by medical staff or even by me. I have no doubt, today, that my gallstones were my body's way of trying to speak to me; begging me to listen; begging me to honour *all* of the parts of me, including my *emotional* body.

It makes sense that I would continue to have these medical issues as I was dissociated, and therefore unable to practice conscious body awareness. The disconnect from my body combined with a belief system that denied Emotional self-awareness was a *Molotov cocktail* of self-destruction. I lived with a surplus of unexpressed fear my entire life, making it more difficult for me to connect with anger and grief as they lived outside the walls of my titanium fortress. I sucked anger up with a smile, or misdirected it, causing harm. I think now of the rhyme, "Sticks and stones…." and how my fear of anger and inability to own it had my body creating stones I seemed to be throwing at myself.

By twenty-one, I was a married mother with my first child. Like the wake from a speedboat, waves of purpose and meaning covered over every ounce of my defended structure, and found the hidden crevices to drain into my thirsty heart. She widened the cracks with her smile. I immediately knew I'd never tire of soaking up this kind of love. My next two children were equally invited and received with overwhelming gratitude and love. I came into this marriage with just the right tools. One might say I was becoming a master mechanic. You know how they say mechanics drive the worst cars? I was pulling out every trick of the trade to keep my body looking showroom ready. But like putting pepper in a radiator, the facade of a healthy marriage was beginning to crumble. The love for my kids was the glue that held me together. No one knew what was happening behind closed doors. I didn't even tell my sister. I felt alone, and manifested deeper loneliness in isolation. I left that marriage with my brilliant eight, six and two year old children. They were filled to the brim with life lessons they would teach me over the following twenty years. I left the holes in the walls of that home behind me. I even left a kidney! Oh yeah, I hadn't mentioned yet that I donated a kidney to a relative of my now ex husband. I felt honoured to play a role in supporting someone's life. No regrets. I do, however, wonder if my act of kindness was also one of self preservation. Fear is held in the kidney. I'd been scared for so long. Perhaps I'd unconsciously concluded that it would be easier to deny my fear if I removed the organ that held it?

I'd been afraid for most of my life. In this Chapter I share the signs and symptoms of unexpressed fear held in the body as listed in Susan Aaron's training manual from her Psychodramatic Bodywork® course. I walk through my extensive list of body breaks and illness and how I connect them to unexpressed emotion I held in my body. I invite you to explore your own body breaks and illness. Have you held unexpressed emotions in your body throughout your lifetime? Can you walk through your *bodytalk*, and develop a deeper understanding of how it speaks to you?

"It's not a matter of "finding yourself" but rediscovering yourself under layers of judgement, doubt and fear."

UNKNOWN

CHAPTER 8: THE DEFIBRILLATOR

Do you believe in divine intervention? Do you believe that everything happens for a reason? Do you believe that there is an energy or force out there that's greater than you, just waiting to guide you when you're able to trust and believe? Until the last few years, I'd be more apt to chalk something up to coincidence, or I'd just say, "Isn't that weird?" I rarely say that now. Today, I see the signs, and I embrace the lessons. I truly believe, as Tony Robbins wrote in his books, that, "Life happens for us, not to us." But I haven't always felt this way.

In the summer of 2018, I decided to peel away layers of myself, both literally and figuratively. I planned to cross the stage in a bodybuilding competition. I should go back a wee bit first, to offer some context. I began a unique form of therapeutic group work in 2013 called *Psychodramatic Bodywork*® with Susan Aaron. Her workshops taught me which organs hold each emotion, and the signs and symptoms of when these emotions are suppressed in the body, rather than released. This learning has been life-changing for me. I had no idea how disconnected I was from my emotions, and how my lack of awareness impacted my physical body. This work had me look back at the abuse I'd experienced and witnessed from childhood, and into my adult life. The awareness that has created my shift, however, was the unveiling of how *I've* treated my own body. Why is this awareness the catalyst for growth and change in my life? Though I can't change what happened to me, I can change how I treat my body moving forward.

Throughout the years, I've endured a multitude of orthopedic tears and breaks. I've suffered from chronic stone growth for which Aaron's work offered a logical explanation. As such, I saw the upcoming bodybuilding competition as a chance to apply the new skills I'd learned from Susan. Bodybuilding requires awareness and engagement of a multitude of muscles in the body. You see, I took the introductory course in Psychodramatic Bodywork® to become a better counselor. I hoped to use these skills to help others. It took me five years of study and work before I truly committed to applying the theories and practice on *myself,* daily. The decision to do the work was important; as was the application of patience for myself and my process. The latter took a *lot* longer.

Prior to the competition, I reached out to an incredible coach and trainer who I had worked with, and for. I told her I wanted to do a fitness competition and she set me up with a 12-month nutrition and training regime. I knew it was going to be hard. I knew it would challenge my relationship with food. Sugar and I had had a lifetime secret love affair riddled with shame and guilt. I'd hoped to cut ties with both. Even though I'd never competed before, as a part-time certified personal trainer and fitness instructor, I knew sculpting my body to reach a competitive level would take mind-body connection. I knew that it would be an emotional healing journey throughout the 12 months leading up to the competition. I had no idea back then what else it was preparing me for.

I knew I would be addressing my closet sugar binging if I wanted to eat like a competitive athlete. I knew this would mean delving deeper into my experiences of childhood sexual abuse, physical abuse, and intimate partner violence; both experienced and witnessed. I had done a lot of work already, *talking* about my experiences of abuse. A lot. I knew this would take me further though. How did I know that something like *meal planning* would have me diving into those dark waters?

Childhood trauma had robbed me of the ability to trust, and armed me with the need to control. When I *talked* about my feelings I had complete control of the words that left my lips. *Feeling* the feelings I talked about, was a whole other can of *whoop ass* I'd been avoiding like the plague. One thing I trusted, however, was the magic of a quick sugar fix. I knew that removing this crutch would rip off a few band-aids. I just knew it.

Applying the tools I'd learned from Susan Aaron forced me to talk less and feel more; step out of my head and into my body. What a terrifying thought for me; much like stepping into the abyss of becoming a writer. But I'm learning to stay in my body and articulate my feelings to make them shareable. It's a personal healing I hadn't anticipated when I decided to write. Much like attending Susan Aaron's first workshop, I started writing with the hope that my story might help others with shared experiences of trauma. I assumed I'd simply tell my story. I'd done so much work to date, but could there be more? Oh yes. I'm quickly learning the universe has bigger plans for me.

I'm learning that the best way to encourage others to dive into the deep waters within themselves is to do likewise. I'm realizing that sharing what I've learned for the purpose of helping others means remaining on my own learning and healing journey too. Kind of beautiful, isn't it? We get to walk through this together.

As such, I'm delving within myself; into the crooks and crevices; a place where pain and fear have called home for too long. Like dirt and dust that collect in the corners of a room, I'm exposing those piles, then sifting through, feeling each particle between my fingers. I'm starting to see how each pile begins to morph into pieces, like that of a puzzle. Suddenly, these piles of irritants, like dirt in the corner of a room that my broom can't reach, become the missing pieces of my story that I've unconsciously longed to know, and now share with you.

Abuse and trauma taught me how to disconnect. Competing would force me to feel my body as I learned to engage each and every muscle. It helped me recognize when I was suppressing emotion. How on earth could training for a fitness competition do that? Fear became an annoying tattletale that gave me no choice but to release emotion if I wanted to be successful at this sport!

Difficulty taking-in and retaining information is one of the symptoms of unexpressed fear. My trainer, Alexa, would show me two movements, watch me do them, and make any necessary corrections. She would walk away, leaving me to complete my sets. For the first several months, I would pick up the weight, and forget nearly *everything* she showed *and* told me!

This happened time and time again. In the beginning, I would ask for reminders, once, maybe twice. When I couldn't remember after a second refresher, I would make something up. I was too embarrassed to tell her I couldn't remember. My embarrassment had nothing to do with my coach. It had everything to do with my inability to feel safe in my vulnerability. So what did I do? I listened to my body and did what it was asking me to do. I was scared, so I released fear! After training, I would get in my car and scream out a song at the top of my lungs! Then I would cry. I cried *a lot!* What changed by inviting these two simple practices into my training program? I started to remember, and required fewer reminders. Feeling more *present* found me embracing and enjoying my entire program, nutrition included.

I was gifted with my incredible coach named Alexa. She had the energy of a thousand horses and the focus of a panther hunting prey when working with a client. Like me, Alexa had no idea that there was a different stage performance she was training me for; perhaps the most horrific event of my life. I couldn't have known how sculpting my body would become the first form of *temporary healthy disconnection* from a scary and painful event that was only months away from happening. The deeper understanding of my muscle anatomy, and targeting single muscle flexion became, and continues to be, a *go to* when I feel the pull to disconnect.

To be honest, I was pretty naive at the time. I k*ind of believed my personal trauma quota had been met.* I felt pretty confident that the only trauma I would experience moving forward was in witnessing and supporting others. Boy, was I wrong. I was wrong that my personal experiences with trauma were over, but I was right about noticing coincidence. I was right in holding the door open, even if just a crack, to discover a connection with a source of guidance that exists beyond the human experience. To this day, I believe that something greater than me led to the decision to compete. Call it an *energy* or a *guide* that knew my capabilities far beyond what I knew to be true within myself at that time. It's as if my *spirit guides* were preparing me for something monumental. I think of the infamous *Footprints in the Sand* poem that speaks to moments in time when we are carried by God.

Margaret Fishback Powers wrote "Footprints" in 1964:

Footprints in the Sand
One night I dreamed I was walking along the beach with the Lord. Many scenes from my life flashed across the sky. In each scene I noticed Footprints in the Sand. Sometimes there were two sets of footprints, and other times there was one only. This bothered me because I noticed that during the low periods of my life, when I was suffering from anguish, sorrow or defeat, I could see only one set of footprints, so I said to the Lord, "You promised me Lord, that if I followed you, you would walk with me always, but I have noticed that during the most trying periods of my life there has only been one set of footprints in the sand. Why, when I needed you most, have you not been there for me?" The Lord replied, "The years when you have seen only one set of footprints, my child, is when I carried you."

I'd been a trauma-informed counselor for seventeen years when I made the decision to compete. I worked mostly with women who had experienced intimate partner violence. I'd come to honour that it was no accident that I was drawn to this sector. I could relate to the kids, because I'd been there. I could relate to the moms because I was there when I started working in that sector in 2001.

Witnessing the courage and strength of hundreds of women and children navigating abuse in their lives, and learning to choose themselves, was incredibly inspiring. Their courage gave *me* courage. I truly felt inspired, on a daily basis, to do hard things. Surrounding myself with brave and resilient women greatly influenced my desire to heal my own wounds. I was ready to do the personal healing work that my year of training for competition would uncover.

Training would offer a mental escape, and align my focus, forcing me to stay connected to my body when unhealthy habits tried to take over. Disconnecting from myself by staying quiet, or stepping into a role that I could hide in had been my *traditional* coping strategies in the past. My physical body suffered during these times of disconnect, and my emotional and mental health suffered as well. My ability to gauge and recognize my own emotions was still underdeveloped. I knew the signs and symptoms of unexpressed emotions at this time, but I was still actively doing daily scans as I had so many layers of fear to move through.

I believe now that a power greater than me was at work back in July 2018. I was led to commit to competing, 5 months before a day that would change the rest of my life. I needed to be well into the practice of connecting with myself so that, as the footprints poem suggests, I could carry myself, and have trust in *spirit* to step in when I was unable to hold my own weight.

My husband, Jeff, and I went to the gym together that day; a regular outing for me. Six months into my training, I was going to the gym twice a day, most days. It was December 29, 2018. This date is engraved in my mind, like a concrete footprint. My competition date would be in July, 2019. I was excited because since his shift from swinging a hammer to sitting at a desk as an Insurance Appraiser, his interest in gym time had disappeared. In spite of that, I've never believed that couples have to have everything in common. Jeff and I are very different, yet something we shared, in addition to our love for our kids, was being fit, and competition. He was a runner when we met. We'd competed in a few trail runs together, and quite a few road races too. My greatest takeaways from those events weren't the free t-shirts or the medals. Rather, it was the times together with him and the drives to and from the races.

On that fateful day, I had a great workout as I always did. The gym was my safe place to push hard and sweat. *"I wish I never went to the gym"* is something nobody ever says, right? On the way home, Jeff said his workout felt sluggish. I assumed he was being hard on himself, and praised him for going. Jeff's a perfectionist, so I thought nothing more about his reported *crappy workout* until about an hour later. I remember him saying he didn't feel well. He said his heart was racing and he felt nauseous. I put my hand on his chest. It felt like his heart was punching the palm of my hand through his skin. I suggested he eat as he hadn't done so since the gym. He agreed since the only thing he'd consumed all day was coffee. So he made himself some soup. While he ate, I Googled his symptoms. Low blood sugar came up as a possibility. I hoped he would feel better after he ate.

The truth is that I was Googling symptoms because I knew something was wrong. I'm not a medical professional; that's my sister, she's a nurse. I'm just Danielle, with my *feelings*. Always trying to get out of my own way so that those feelings may better guide me. On this day, I just wanted my feelings to be wrong.

But my feeling was accurate; something was wrong. Something was very wrong. Jeff told me he was going to be sick. We'd been together for seventeen years at this time. I'd never seen Jeff vomit before. I didn't see it on this day either because he was in the bathroom with the door shut. I just heard him. I didn't dare barge in. Seventeen years together, but there were a lot of intimate moments we had never shared. I called him through the door.

"Jeff! Are you ok?"

"No! I'm not," he answered.

I asked him a question, knowing the answer already.

"Do you think you need to go to the hospital?"

In total shock, I heard him respond, "Yes."

In seventeen years, Jeff's only visit to the hospital was following our decision to stop at five children. A quick visit with the family doctor to treat his annual sinus infection was the only other medical intervention I'd seen with Jeff. *I* was the one who knew the orthopedic surgeons, the obstetricians, the gastroenterologist, the donor surgeon. *I* was the one with a closet full of knee braces and crutches. *I* birthed the babies. *I* got the injuries that warranted countless trips to the hospital, affording me a medical file a foot thick.

Jeff was the one that picked up the aftercare medication. *Jeff* did the over the speed limit drive to the hospital while I was in labour. *Jeff* followed the ambulance after yet *another* break on the soccer pitch. That was *Jeff's* role. Not mine.

The roles changed on December twentyninth, 2018. Jeff was in the car before I had my shoes on. Calling an ambulance was not a thought as we were just an eleven minute drive away, according to Google, to the hospital. That's assuming you're driving the speed limit. *"Drive the car, Danielle."* That's all I thought. Pulling out of the driveway and down our street, our youngest son (eleven) came riding on his bike to meet us. I stopped the car, and took a breath as I put my window down.

"Hey buddy!" I said with a smile and a prayer that he would not see my terror.

"Your brother's in the house. Put your bike away, and head inside. Dad and I are heading out, and I'll let you both know when we'll be back." I have no idea how I put those sentences together. It was like forces beyond me took over, and put my speech together for me. I had no idea when we would be back.

"Drive the car, Danielle."

At the end of our street, I called the hospital. To be honest, I had no idea what I was going to say. I had no idea what was happening. I just knew it was bad, but I had no idea what *IT* was. I didn't even know exactly what Jeff was experiencing because he wasn't talking. He had his hand on his chest, and held an eerie silence that pierced my ears with horrific fear. The hospital answered, and I heard myself saying,

"... My husband is forty four, his brother died of a heart attack at forty three and I think he's having a heart attack. Please be ready for us when we get there!"

The voice responded telling me Jeff would be assessed when we arrived, and seen in order of priority. I heard myself cutting her off like a machete would a blade of grass.

"My husband is forty four, his brother died of a heart attack at forty three and I think he's having a heart attack!! He is a PRIORITY!!"

Then I hung up.

Drive the car, Danielle.

How could I explain to an emergency service worker that despite my absence of medical training, I *knew* I was bringing in the most acute patient they would see that day? In fact, Jeff would receive a level of care never given to *anyone* before in this hospital by a doctor who had only taught a new procedure to EMS students using mannequins.

After hanging up from the hospital, Jeff spoke for the first time since we got in the car. I had stopped at a set of lights and he threw a monotone dart that stated, "Drive through the fucking lights."

I couldn't believe what I was hearing. I was *terrified* but there was no time to feel it.

Drive the car, Danielle.

I made another call to the person who had been with me since the beginning, my sister. Even if she didn't know what to do, being scared with her felt better than being scared alone.

She picked up the phone and greeted me with her usual, "Hey Sis!"

Tina has a unique ability to hug you with her voice. It's as if she lifts you onto a stage with the spotlight already set to showcase you, and she has seated herself front row center. I felt a wave of relief when she answered. Guilt quickly joined, because I knew my words would scare her. I never wanted to scare my sister. We grew up together and I knew she'd experienced enough fear to last several lifetimes.

"Ok Sis." I started. "I need you to listen to me carefully please."

I've never started a call like this with my sister before. I knew I needed to be clear with my words.

I continued with, "With the exception of fire, or bomb, what do I need to tell the hospital so they understand the severity of the patient I'm bringing in? I think Jeff might be having a heart attack."

This was the second time I heard these words come out of my mouth. I felt like I was in a bad dream.

I'm not a stranger to nightmares. I've had nightmares where I realized it was just a dream. I could shut my eyes tight and say out loud, "It's just a dream, it's just a dream." This would cause me to wake up. I really wanted this drive to be a dream. I wanted to close my eyes tight, and wake up. Instead, my voice kept telling me,

"Drive the car, Danielle."

I kept my phone on speaker, as my Bluetooth wasn't connected. I started naming my location by street names and landmarks. I knew she was listening. I knew I was alone, but much less alone now with my sis on the other end of the phone. "I've just turned on to Larry St., coming up to the park on my right." I told my sister.

There was a three-way stop by the park, and Jeff again told me, "Dont stop." This time, his words came through gritted teeth.

As I drove through the stop sign, I heard myself tell my sister, "This is really bad."

My sister, the nurse, answered the phone as my sis, and despite my request for the nurse, my sister remained my sis. She later shared with me that she dropped the phone. She said she panicked. I felt that would have been a pretty normal response from a sister, considering the situation. What I later learned is that my quick-thinking, brilliantly huge-hearted nephew took charge. This allowed my sister to stay *my sis.* He called 911. He stayed on the phone with EMS while listening to me through my sister's phone. He heard everything; every detail. He relayed all the information to the 911 dispatcher. In addition to landmarks I was passing, I was also providing detailed updates about what was happening to Jeff. Very detailed. I thought I was speaking to my sister, the nurse. I didn't know my sister wasn't on the phone with me anymore because my phone had dropped too. Actually, it slid off my lap when I slammed on the brakes.

After driving through the 3-way stop, I had just four more sets of lights to go before the hospital. We were so close! The next set of lights were fast approaching, but turning yellow. "Shit!" I no sooner cursed that I felt Jeff grab and quickly release my arm.

"I'm gonna pass out." He seemed to be forcing the words out.

I set my hand on his leg, "Just close your eyes and breathe, Hon. I'm going to get you to the hospital, I promise." I had *no* idea where those words of comfort came from. *I was terrified!* These were the last words we shared before his heart stopped. I heard a *thud.* I couldn't look.

"Drive the car, Danielle! Drive the car, Danielle!"

Time seemed to slow at this point. I wish it hadn't. There would be less space to hold the memories. I wanted this to be a dream. I wanted to wake up. I was forced to slam on the brakes as the light was turning from yellow to red, as another car entered the intersection. The abrupt stop forced Jeff's lifeless body forward, then back. I looked just as Jeff's head flew back. His lifeless gray eyes met mine. I was alone. "He's *gone…*he's had a heart attack." I couldn't believe what I heard myself saying. "Oh my God, Oh my God, Oh my God!". I'm sure there was a lot more, but that's all I recall.

"Drive the car, Danielle! Drive the car, Danielle!"

When the light turned green, I made the turn. "Just three more sets of lights to go." I quickly counted in my head.

I continued to state the landmarks out loud so I wouldn't drive off the road. I remember putting the passenger window down at the second last set of lights. I couldn't believe it was another red light. I remember yelling out the window to the car beside me who's windows were up. I remember a couple looking my way and laughing. Perhaps they thought I was bellowing out my favourite song on a Saturday afternoon, three days before New Year's Eve. That makes sense. It's a fun time of year for many, after all. I wasn't though. I wanted to ask them to help me. I don't know how they could have. I was so taken by fear, the request seemed fitting.

"Do I pull over? Do I pull Jeff out of the car and start CPR? Do I keep driving? Then I heard myself again,

"Drive the car, Danielle."

Thank God the final two sets of lights were green. I drove as fast as I could, continuing to shout out where I was. By this time my phone was on the floor near my feet. I wailed on my horn as I pulled into the emergency carport. I put my car in park, and ran to the doors yelling,

"My husband's in the car! He's not breathing!"

When the emergency doors opened, time slowed again. I watched as a team of hospital staff flocked to Jeff's aid like the perfect football huddle, yet moving in slow motion. I could see their mouths moving, offering direction to each other, but the sounds were muffled in my ears. They pulled him out of my car. He was missing a shoe. They started CPR right there on the concrete outside the emergency doors. I *was* in a nightmare. There was no squeezing my eyes shut and waking up from this one though. My legs felt like cement. I felt even more helpless somehow with the emergency crew working on him. My role of driving the car had ended, and there was no role for me left to play.

The emergency nurse rode the gurney through the automatic doors as she continued CPR on Jeff. The doors shut behind him, and I was alone again. I stood there, the passenger side door still open. Jeff's other shoe was there. I was asked to move my car. Move my car? I asked to be accompanied as I parked because I was afraid I'd forgotten how to drive. A member of the hospital staff came with me and I parked the car. I don't remember the walk back to the room where Jeff was being vigorously worked on.

There was a team of medical staff trying to revive my husband. Even without the medical knowledge, I knew it wasn't working. It was obvious they were working on a lifeless body. I stood and watched as they worked tirelessly on him. It was like witnessing the inner workings of an older Century inner city clock. So much was happening and none of it made sense to me. But I had full trust they were trying everything. I watched as they used the defibrillator. I watched how they worked together, perfectly aligned like the gears within a clock; remarkably in sync. They continued to use the defibrillator.

I heard what appeared to be the doctor leading the team say, "Let's go again."

I remember wondering how long I'd been standing there. One nurse approached me, then another, and again another, asking if I wanted to sit down. Had I been there long enough that I should have needed to sit? That can't be good, can it?

"Is this really happening?" I asked the first nurse. She put her hand on my shoulder and said nothing.

"Is this really fuckin' happening?" I heard myself plead to the second nurse. *Who talks like that at a time like this?* I remember thinking that to myself as I heard the curse words shooting from my lips like bullets at a gun range.

The next thing I remember was seeing automatic doors slide open to reveal my sister. Time slowed yet again as she made her way to me. You see, my sister lived twenty-five minutes from the hospital. I ended the call with her when I arrived. She was still at home. Jeff's heart stopped before we arrived at the hospital. Suddenly, reality smacked me in the face. Jeff stopped breathing more than twenty-five minutes ago! They had already used the defibrillator 5 or 6 times by the time she arrived.

I heard myself say, "Sis, this isn't good, is it?" My sister would never say anything to hurt me. She would do anything to see me avoid pain.

She said, "No Sis, it isn't good."

I stood there numb. I felt nothing and everything. Looking back, I know I'd felt this way before. There was an uncanny similarity to when I was five years old.

I was in the living room of my apartment staring at my biological father and a police officer in one corner, my sobbing mother and sister in the other. There was blood and hair on the floor. There was blood on my father's hands. I believe I left myself that day when I was five. The only way out was to leave myself behind. I ran to my father. It was the right choice as a child. It kept me safe. I think I shrunk myself until I was like a grain of sand. My body, like a shell, empty; free to be inhabited by the role of my choosing to move forward. Free to be what anyone needed me to be. Tucking myself away within my shell gave me a feeling of safety and control. If I could control, I'd never be left in that kind of terror again. Or so I thought.

How could it be that over forty years later, I would find myself just outside the open doors of a trauma room, feeling like I did when I was five?

Has my life come full circle to this pivotal moment?

Had my work on connecting my mind and body been preparation for what I was witnessing? Had I been led to the work I'd been doing by spirit so I could see an alternative to remaining that grain of sand, and hiding?

Had I been preparing to unshrink myself?

Was this my moment to take the reins from control and fear, and trust in my connection to self and spirit?

My sister had my right arm tucked-in tight to her body. The two of us stood, pressed together like crazy glue. If one of us lost our footing we would surely take the other down. How fitting that this tragic and pivotal moment in my life was held and witnessed so brilliantly by my sister? I don't know what she was thinking. I don't remember anything else she said as we watched the medical team continue to shock his body. I do know that I stayed in my body this time. Here I stood, fixated on my husband's lifeless shell; I could feel my heart racing. I knew my legs were shaking. In this moment, it's as if Jeff and I were standing on opposite ends of a lifeline continuum. Jeff: leaving his body. Me; landing in mine. I was present. I hadn't run. It was as if each defib administered a shock into Jeff's heart, and into my essence; in unison. I was experiencing the most bizarre dichotomy of Jeff leaving his body, and me coming back into mine.

Looking back, I realize that the big difference between this trauma and what I witnessed at the age of five, was knowing I wasn't alone. When I was five, I didn't have that. I felt alone. I had to make the only decision there was to survive. There were no other options when I was five. I had to have control, in order to be safe. When I stood watching Jeff, I could feel him drifting away, and I was scared. But! I was able to be present because I didn't feel alone. I could *feel* my sister with me this time, unlike in our childhood. I believe I could feel the presence of my sister because I could also *feel* the presence of spirit, of God, of a Divine presence that was there holding me along with my sister. I knew I wasn't alone.

I thought about what I would tell our kids; how I would hold them in their grief. I thought about the calls I'd have to make. I was fully present. I was terrified, but I knew I was safe, and capable.

I was so aware that I was able to hear the words, "We got him back!"

I felt just a whisper of relief, as I knew Jeff's survival was still uncertain. His heart had stopped beating, and his brain had been without oxygen for almost half an hour before they shocked him back. He received a single defibrillation three times, and double defibrillation using two machines an additional four times. Days later, I was greeted by the Doctor who led the team that worked on him in the Emergency Department. He explained the 'best of the best' *just happened* to be on shift that afternoon when I pulled in with Jeff. He referred to them as, "The dream team."

He told me he *taught* this method of using two defibrillators to his EMS students, but had *never* performed it on a human body, until Jeff. In fact, this was the first time this method had *ever* been used at this hospital. He said the staff that was present that day was the best there was, and his recovery after receiving a stent, and a medically-induced coma was nothing short of a miracle.

Was it a miracle? Was it divine intervention that kept me on the road, and helped me deliver Jeff safely to the hospital after his heart stopped? I'm completely convinced I was accompanied by God that afternoon that Jeff had a heart attack in the car with me on route to the hospital. I believe the months of training for my competition leading up to the heart attack had my mind and body more deeply connected and capable of staying present in the crisis. The physical training kept me from dissociating in the crisis, and allowed me to trust in my abilities to ask for help and honour my feelings rather than deny and suppress them.

"To heal is to touch with love that which we previously touched with fear."

STEPHEN LEVINE

CHAPTER 9: GRIEF

The impact of unexpressed grief would manifest itself in my final year of high school. Grief was where I felt *most* vulnerable. As the fear became insurmountable, my suppressed grief shifted into countless x-rays, MRI's, and surgeries. This ran unabated from the age of eighteen, well into my 40s.

I mentioned the impacts on the body of unexpressed grief earlier. As I recap, and share the impacts on *my* body, I invite you to think about *your* relationship with grief and sadness. Is it easy for you to cry? Do you welcome support from others when you're sad, or are you more inclined to suck it up? If one tear escapes, do you feel like you have just *balled your eyes out*? If this describes you, I can relate!

Here's a fun fact: For hundreds of years, the Chinese, and other Asian cultures, have hired professional mourners (also called wailers) to attend funerals. The more wailing that's heard, the greater honour is brought to the family of the deceased. The hired wailers help the families connect with their grief and allow everybody an opportunity to cry unabashedly.

What this tells me is that I'm not alone in my struggle to identify my emotions and to free them. I've since found that this method of watching a sad movie or TV series can be a magnificent tool for releasing sadness, without having to focus on a part of my own sad story. I can cry for the lead character

Meredith, when her husband dies. I can cry with the actors on my television screen without the risk of my own judgements and instinctive survivalist blocking techniques holding me back. My tears are pulled from my personal reservoir from any time in my life that I've been sad and unable to release.

When we cry, fluid is released from the body. Tears fall from the eyes, and our noses run. The body gets warm and often sweating occurs when releasing sadness and grief. Simply put, when we feel sad, our bodies produce and release fluid. When you feel sad, and don't cry, what do you think happens to the fluid? When you feel sad a lot, and rarely cry; again, what happens to all of that fluid? The fluid is held in the body, and can create weakness in the joints and illness related to the immune system, the lungs and heart.

For me, unexpressed grief manifested itself in many orthopedic injuries. I had my first of several orthopedic surgeries at eighteen, after a meniscal tear in my right knee. By my forties, I would have three more surgeries in my right knee, a plate and 6 pins in my left ankle, and a torn rotator cuff in my right shoulder. All of these injuries occurred playing sports or fitness training.

I felt pain and weakness in these areas, and told myself, "Suck it up!"

I ignored the warnings from my body. I listened to my internal dialogue that told me, *only the weak get injured.* "Train harder," I told myself.

Despite the hurt I'd caused my physical body in sports, I now recognize the brilliance of the roles I created as an athlete. I was able to safely release some of my emotions without feeling vulnerable. As a young athlete, I could be drenched in sweat. And if tears came, no one would know. As a teenager, I let my anger out on the opposing team, *a lot*. I was perceived as an aggressive player. Looking back, I found safety in that persona. I didn't feel tough inside, but I sure enjoyed the safety that the aggressive role provided me. I wonder if I made anyone feel as afraid as I was? I hope not. I let out a lot of my anger in my teenage years.

Later in life, as a certified personal trainer, spin instructor, soccer coach, and adult soccer player, I let go of, *'Danielle, the Poor Sport.'* I seamlessly replaced her with, *'Danielle, the machine.'*

I continued to push my body with a tremendous lack of respect and care. I was like the stereotypical mechanic driving the worst beater car down the street. I was a trainer, an athlete, a coach, a mother of five, and a counselor. I chose leadership roles; encouraging and supporting others with love and nurturing, and strengthening their connections to themselves and others. I'd always felt these roles I played helped other people, and gave me a feeling of worth and value. Back then, my worth was measured by how much value others found in my acts of service.

But feeling chosen came at a great cost to my body. I could continue to 'grin and bear it,' or learn how to listen to my body. Before I knew what I know now, I chose to plow through. I realize how the roles I created to stay safe were both a blessing and a curse. Each role afforded me new connections and relationships while keeping my vulnerability safely masked.

But I was always scared.

The connections I developed were guarded, and limited. My past had taught me that fear was a warning that someone was going to get hurt; and that *someone* was often me. I now understand I had to learn the difference between feeling *fear* and being *unsafe*. When I gained that wisdom, I could strip away the costumes I wore. I could reveal my true self to the world.

Understanding that **fear is a *feeling*, and not always a warning that I'm unsafe,** took a lot of work for me! I had to slow the heck down. I may admire and be inspired by the turtle, but there's a glaring dissimilarity: I don't *like* to go slowly! A turtle appears to have a brilliant wisdom that guides its movement and its pace. The path one travels seems intentional, to me. Turtles seem to have a *knowing*, or a *trust* that they are moving in the right direction. I've had to work extremely hard to embrace *my own knowing*. Feeling full comfort in stillness is very much a work in progress for me. But I'm committed!

The part of the turtle I have always resonated with is its tough exterior. Like the turtle, my perception of an athlete was that they were strong. I grew up watching my big brother, the athlete. I carried his equipment and I listened to him tell me what it took to be great at sport. To me, Tony appeared confident, disciplined, and physically strong; even fearless. Feeling afraid all the time had been exhausting for me. I wanted to be chosen by my brother. And yet, I can't help but wonder if I believed the only way that could happen, was if I too were strong and fearless?

I wanted my own costume of strength and fearlessness. Looking back, I'm truly amazed how early I disconnected from my body, and became hyper-focussed on how the world saw me.

I was immersed in developing, even *mastering* the art of deflection, and cleverly masked it as a drive for connection. When you're an athlete, a coach, or even a mother of five, these roles can be used to mask real trauma. That's because there's a degree of control in each of these positions that doesn't always require a two-way divulgence of what's really going on behind the mask. This was my perception of strength beyond the physical. It was defined as the absence of needs and fear. Disconnecting from myself allowed me to easily stand in the role of the strong and fearless.

I can see now that I told myself a story about my brother based on how safe I felt when I was with him. I wanted to feel safe. All. The. Time. I think I believed that if I could be *just like him*, he would always choose me, and I'd always feel safe. I watched him and listened; I hung on his every word, and behaviour. Yes, I'd pinned a lot of my hopes on a young man in his teens, but I needed to borrow his strength for a time, until I developed a true, authentic strength within myself. I needed to learn how to choose myself. The pain and injuries that came with pushing my body to the limit and emulating my brother Tony eventually taught me to turn inward. That's where the healing would begin.

Today, my brother and I share a mutual respect and admiration for one another. We bathe in humility when praising each other. He has even named *me*, 'the wise little sister,' which still makes me blush. I'm able to admire my brother's charisma and knowledge, and also see my own. **I can do this having moved from complete self-abandonment in the relentless need for control, to my final resting place of reconnecting with myself.** Growing up, I could never have imagined my brother wanting or needing anything from me. I took direction from him as a devout Christian would follow scripture from the Bible.

If Tony told me to run around the block, I would run around the block as fast as I could.

When I stopped, he would say, "Go again, Danielle!"

And I would. I ran until either my legs gave out, or I would vomit. I was about ten or eleven then. I felt chosen by my brother. I found a role I was good at, too. This role would both serve and harm me for many years to come.

I'd learned how to quickly identify who I needed to be in order to please other people. I was able to develop a relationship with my brother. I, however, brought the limitations in order to stay safe. Carrying past trauma had my essence bound and tied-up in a closet. It would be many years before I would finally believe I could safely let my *inner self* out. I had locked myself up. I'd unconsciously committed to filling my empty shell with whatever others needed.

Oh the irony! **I had such a desire for control. I was like a robot. But, being what others needed me to be meant having *no* access to my own remote. The price of self-abandonment was high.**

I could be anyone for everyone, and nobody for myself.

I would suffer years riddled with sports injuries and surgeries. I endured ligament tears, breaks and even the removal of organs before taking out the metaphorical earbuds and listening to the painful messages coming from my body. The more I stepped into a role that met the needs of others, and hid my fear, the more I silenced and ignored my physical and emotional self. During the formative years of my life, I would sit back, watch and listen; always figuring out how to stay safe, yet also be chosen. Holding in grief was injurious to my physical and mental health, and directly impacted my ability to connect with others.

"I sat with my anger long enough, until she told me her real name was grief."

UNKNOWN

CHAPTER 10: EAT IT OR WEAR IT

I was six years old, and, up to that point, having a Dad hadn't been anything like what was portrayed in movies or on TV commercials; but I still really wanted one.

When we moved away to escape my biological dad, our new home came with the beautiful front door and a man that I would soon call, "Dad." He was unassuming in height. He didn't wear a crown, but his authority reigned like a king over his kingdom. He would tell us, "A man's home is his castle." And he would quickly show us that *our* ranking behind closed doors was anything but royalty. He had brilliant blue eyes like his parents', but I rarely saw them twinkle. My new dad bought sugar cereal, sometimes, and called me 'Blunder Buckets,' or 'Squirt.' I felt chosen when he used these endearing Irish slangs. Soon after I met him, I learned that as long as I did just what he said, I was safe.

I now realize that my stepfather was someone I never *tried* to emulate. Unlike my relationship with Tony, there was no drive to be just like my stepfather. I was years into my personal work before I recognized my need for control. I grew-up feeling like my stepfather controlled *everything,* even my relationship with food.

He controlled how I ate, what I ate, and how much I ate.

How is that possible?

He accomplished that with five small words, spoken at the dinner table.

I remember being in a restaurant, eating one of the few foods that my selective palette allowed me, especially away from home. My palette was restricted to chicken fingers, egg salad sandwiches, onion rings, and chocolate milk. When handed a menu, I would anxiously scan the items until I located one of these fine foods. A blanket of relief would envelop my body when I found one. "Phew," I would sigh to myself. Not only did I feel confident eating these foods, I knew I was less likely to use my utensils incorrectly, as these simple foods allowed for the use of my hands. My sister, the forever *food connoisseur*, loved to experiment with *different* foods.

I was in awe of her courage at a restaurant. She would order *any* item that seemed to tantalize her curious taste buds! I would wonder, "Does she have amnesia?" Perhaps she decided the outcome was inevitable, so she might as well order whatever struck her fancy. *Carpe diem*, right? Her bravery scared me though. It felt like watching someone *knowingly* walk into a burning forest. I felt powerless.

 "I'd like peppermint tea please." My brave sister would request.

The warning followed from my Stepfather. "Are you going to drink all of it?"

"Yes." My Sister responded with an innocent excitement.

Having never consumed a specialty tea before, my sister loaded her peppermint tea with milk and sugar. I thought we'd all finished, when my stepfather's voice silenced our departure like the pounding of a gavel.

"Eat it or wear it." He pointed to my sister's unfinished cup of tea.

I watched, frozen in horror, as my stepfather splashed the cup of tea in my sister's face.

She didn't budge an inch.

None of us did.

I remember watching the tea dripping off the tips of her eyelashes and nose. I don't remember how anyone in the restaurant reacted. I just remember the silence.

It was deafening.

"Ok then. Time to go." My stepfather broke the silence with a tone that seemed to have no recollection of the horror we had just experienced. We walked to the car, and drove home. Nothing was said again about what just happened. My sister and I never spoke of it until about 15 years later.

We continued to use silence to nurture the shame embedded in our family secrets.

As you might imagine, my relationship with food has been tumultuous at times. I was well into my adult life before I honoured my trauma around food, and began healing it. I struggled for years to acknowledge how scared I had been.

"How could I be so impacted by what I'd witnessed, but never *personally* experienced?" I would ask myself.

As a trauma-informed counselor today, I no longer ask this question of myself or others having *witnessed* abuse, or trauma. Dr Gabor Mate refers to trauma as the response to the event, not the actual event.

Bearing in mind the *eat it or wear it* experience, I absolutely agree with Mate's theory. As I put the pieces of my past together, I wonder if I took my stepfather's statement as a true question as opposed to his *usual* rhetorical sarcasm.

Eat it or wear it? Perhaps I chose to *eat it*. Perhaps I ate my feelings instead of wearing them. Perhaps I ate my pain instead of wearing it. Had I stuffed my essence instead of sharing it? Was it a question I'd answered rather than a statement I'd contemplated, all these years? Did I choose to devour every crumb of myself, using the tongue and saliva of fear and control?

How my Stepfather treated my sister taught me a lot about staying safe and being chosen in this new home. I listened carefully to my stepfather's beliefs and how he responded to my older siblings and my mom. It's amazing how watching someone else get hit had me feeling the sting on my own cheek. That pain morphed into guilt and shame as I got older. But the violence I witnessed taught me how to avoid being targeted. As a result, I held guilt and shame, for much of my life, for not protecting my big sister. I felt guilty for not standing up for her. Working through these layers of childhood trauma, I clearly see how Tina, my big sister, protected *me*.

My stepfather taught me other things too. He taught me that how you appear in your wedding photo was how you needed to stay if you wanted your marriage to work.

When I showed him the proofs from the photographer after my first wedding, he took the photo in his hand, and said, "See how you look in this picture? This is who your husband married. Remember that. This is how you need to look."

This lesson validated an existing belief that creating roles that suited the needs of others would keep me safe and chosen. It also fueled my sense of body image, and the unhealthy relationship I had with food, stemming from the fear of wearing it.

When he drank, I felt like hunted prey. I pulled out each and every ninja-like movement I could think of. I would maneuver through the house swiftly while holding my breath. Like a squirrel preparing for winter, I would gather my kettle, tea bags, a cup of milk and sugar and take them to my room. My ninja skills proved useful for my many trips to the washroom, walking on my tip toes.

There were times when I drew attention to myself en route to the kitchen for a refill. I'd be struck by his sword of sarcasm, poisoned at the tip by a rye and coke. I would never respond. I wouldn't dare. Looking back, it's not that we were *told* we weren't allowed to go to the bathroom. That rule was never *spoken*. What my sister and I did know, however, is if we interrupted their Friday night dinner in any way, we were yelled at. The rest of the night I would hear yelling, and my mother being verbally 'put back in her place.'

The next day would be like nothing had happened. Not a word would be spoken about the night before. The yelling would be replaced by silence. That kind of quiet was anything but peaceful. It was, in fact, extremely suspenseful. It was like the infamous shower scene in the movie *Psycho*. You knew it was coming: Any second the shower curtain would be whipped open! Waiting for it made the hair on the back of your neck stand up.

The morning-after *stillness* pierced my ears.

Putting my experiences that are riddled with crisis and chaos into writing, has been both healing and enlightening. I'm developing a deeper understanding and compassion for the discomfort I can experience in stillness. **Growing up, my *normal* was a constant vibration of anticipation felt in my body.** If my nervous system was a movie, the title might be '*The Sixth Sense*.' I was unsure of what was happening; yet, I was always trying to predict the scariest parts. This could be the title of my life if not for the introduction to Psychodramatic Bodywork®, and Susan Aaron. Had I never learned the signs and symptoms of fear, anger and grief, I would have remained in a perpetual state of fear. My body would continue to have experienced inflammation, breaks, and illness. The awareness of why I feel familiar in the presence of crisis and chaos encourages me to make more time for peace and quiet. This allows for the shift from my *familiar* to continue.

For those of you walking through my story with me, I highly recommend you consider putting your memoir in writing. Just like me, *you* **have a powerful story to tell** to yourself first! Putting your story in writing, reciting a poem or a song that honours a life experience offers new perspectives and healing. Over the years, I have encouraged women and youth I've worked with to share their stories. I've had the honour of witnessing folks share what they've put in writing with me. I've had the words read to me, spoken through tears, and I've even had some stories shared through song. Afterwards, the storytellers shared that they felt empowered having given voice to their pain, and felt validated in their resilience.

Amazingly, I've come full circle after viewing an ad on Facebook for a workshop presented by *Working Writers Co.* Two brilliant humans, both writers, editors, and Mindset Coaches, providing support to anyone wishing to write a book. I'm now able to live the experience of many of the folks I've helped by telling *my story* with wonderful support. Working with both Working Writers Co. and my fellow peer writers has me feeling surrounded by a team of cheerleaders. We've come to feel like a *chosen* family where we can heal the wounding we experienced in our families of origin.

I feel empowered to explore every nook and cranny of my silenced body and give it voice!

Initially, I thought that characterizing my stepfather would be hard because it meant reliving painful memories. But at this moment, I'm bathing in my own epiphanies. I'm recognizing the deeper layers of my story as well as the stories I've made-up about who I am. There are deeper layers of truth that have my heart both racing and singing. I feel like the conductor just waved his baton to the orchestra, inside my body.

What I discovered characterizing my stepfather, is that I adopted my stepfather's sense of control. Imagine that: the very aspect of his personality I feared the most is what I ended-up adopting. Incredible! This epiphany of mine continues to unfold as I see how controlling my emotions and my environment kept me safe. I also find myself wondering, did my biological father and my stepfather recognize their need for control? I wonder if they had any understanding of the connection between *their* childhood trauma and the need for control? Perhaps like me, they equated control with safety?

I see the brilliance in the roles I created as a child, and the ones I presented in my adult life. All of my roles have been helpful. Today, I embrace the freedom of letting go of the roles, as my need for safety no longer exists. I see how holding *them* would be holding *me* hostage moving forward. The roles have become more harmful than helpful. I understand that I sought control, and safety through food which has proven more harmful in my adult life. **This Chapter offers a prime example of the impact of witnessed abuse on the bystander.**

"Trauma is not what happens to you, but what happens inside you as a result of what happened to you."

DR. GABOR MATE

CHAPTER 11: ANGER

I've always been passionately intrigued hearing and exploring the stories that women share. I've felt honoured witnessing the struggles and the breakthroughs. I imagine my own experiences of trauma helped to create a safe space for many women as they shared their stories and their feelings. The help was mostly *intuitive.* I kept my personal experiences of trauma to *myself* for many years. I didn't recognize the mutually beneficial experience that came with a position of holding space for others. Even if I had known the value, I wasn't willing to relinquish my guarded gate of control that held my emotions hostage.

When I became a counselor, I viewed my role as one-directional. I created a space for women to use their voices. The result was that they heard themselves and continued their personal work as I witnessed. I didn't understand, nor would I have been willing to relinquish control long enough in the beginning to allow the mutual exchange of giving and receiving that currently occurs during sessions with clients. I found comfort in seeing the desk between myself and the folks I was supporting. I bet that sounds arrogant, right? I can see how it might be. The truth is, I sat on the opposite side of arrogance, just as I sat on the other side of the desk from my clients. I sat there because I was scared. I was afraid that if I sat closer, if I removed the desk from between us, they would see that I'm just a frightened woman with little to offer.

I didn't have trust in myself, or the gifts I have. I trusted in my *clients'* abilities to heal and actively embrace their brilliance, I just didn't trust in *my own*. I needed to trust in myself to release control. It's no wonder I felt so familiar working in a shelter setting. Women accessing shelter services have had their trust broken by intimate partners, by family, and by broken systems. Perhaps it was a divine force that led me to immerse my body in a familiar energy with courageous women healing long enough to hold the mirror up to myself that I was working hard to hold up for them. It wasn't arrogance that kept me from removing the desk, it was fear, and a lack of self worth.

I'd been a counselor in a women's shelter for eleven years before I registered for my first Psychodramatic Bodywork® course. After completing the introduction, l decided to take the intermediate course.

This course taught the *blocking mechanisms* that interfere with the expression of emotions. Imagine my shock when I learned my *blocking style* was called a TW/GB, or, *Total Wall/Great big controller* when in *disharmony*?! When in *harmony*, these acronyms stand for *Trusting Wholeness* and *Gentle Boldness*. Initially, I only heard '*the controller*', and I didn't like that at all! I had *a lot* of work to do!

Without delving too deep into the teachings of Psychodramatic Bodywork®, it's important that I share what I learned that made so much sense to me. The trauma I experienced in my life and how I'd survived it had directly impacted my body. **Psychodramatic**

Bodywork® taught me how to listen to my body and understand the messages.

I've been able to map my journey of emotional suppression through my sports injuries and my organ removals. GB referenced the gallbladder Meridian, the organ in which we hold anger, along with the liver. Growing up, witnessing so many unhealthy expressions of anger, taught me to hold-in my own. Years of holding-in anger had my gallbladder overloaded, resulting in an overproduction of stones.

It was fascinating when I learned that my mom had her gallbladder removed as well. Medical doctors named genetics as the root cause. Really? *Two* women experience years of abuse resulting in the suppression of anger, and *both* develop an illness in the organ said to hold anger. *Coincidence?*

It wasn't until I learned by first witnessing then releasing, with support, my own anger that I experienced relief. I've not had a spasm in my bile duct since starting this work. Having reconnected with my body and having learnt how to listen to it, I now notice the early signs that I'm holding-in anger. Just under my ribs on my right hand side, I will feel a dull ache and some tenderness when I press on that area. Today, that signals my need to release anger. The simplicity in this practice is brilliant to me. I don't need to talk about it, I just need to feel it, and release it.

Here's a quick practice you may put yourself through if you're feeling stress and/or body pain that may be associated with unexpressed anger. See if it helps relieve it!

Take a deep breath.

As you exhale, feel both feet firmly planted on the ground.

Close your eyes, and scan your body from head to toe as you continue to breathe.

Identify any places in your body you feel pain in at this moment. Breathe.

Do you feel tension in your jaw? Do you feel tired? Breathe.

Do you often chew gum?

Have you been getting sharp headaches behind your eyes?

When you gently press just under your right ribs, does it feel tender?

Have you had any issues with digestion, or acid reflux? Breathe.

If any of these symptoms describe what you're experiencing, you *may* have some unexpressed anger. These symptoms are all your body's way of letting you know. Emotions are energy. Energy is meant to move through our bodies, not gather in a stagnant space. Feeling anger is healthy. Unexpressed anger *can* be harmful to your body, and potentially to others if it leaks out unconsciously as sarcasm, or as an uncontrollable blast.

So, what can you do when you recognize you have unexpressed anger in your body causing discomfort or pain? Release it! Move it out of your body! Go for a walk, or a run. Kneel in front of your couch, use two clenched fists and punch a pillow until you fatigue. You *will* get tired, even when anger has you seeing red! Write an angry letter, and burn or tear it up after.

Emotions are clear and clean energy. We allow emotional toxicity to grow in our bodies when we hold in, ignore, consciously or unconsciously, our feelings. There are other methods of emotional release work that can be done *when facilitated by trained supports.* It is possible for pain to leave the body immediately following a release. Or, it may take several releases. Release work may be used as a supportive modality of healing alongside other healing methods including Western Medical interventions.

I recently supported a gentleman releasing his unexpressed anger during a private session. He presented with pain in two areas of the body associated with unexpressed anger. He sat down for what was only our second time together. I'd already learned that he wasn't a fan of confrontation. He shared that abuse was part of his childhood. He wore a suit of leadership in the business world, and his *people pleaser* robe behind closed doors.

He started to share a story as he settled into his chair. "I want to tell you something before we start our work together today."

He'd soon learn that his body had already started to warm up before he sat down.

"I've been so fuckin frustrated with my neighbour! He broke my fence, and six months later still hasn't fixed it!" His face turned multiple shades of pink as he spoke.

It fuels my soul to witness someone expressing an emotion they work so hard to hold in. I can relate, of course! I was on the edge of my seat as he told me the email he'd sent his neighbour that morning. He read it to me. The letter was clear and concise as was the direction for the neighbour to pay up! My client got so fired up telling his story, I knew he was ready to let his body complete the tale. I led him over to the stand-up tackle dummy.

"Plant your feet firmly, eyes open, clench your fists, aim for the top, and let out any sound that wants to come!"

He dove into this foreign experience *with all four feet*, and his body erupted with the fury of a volcano.

Here's what you don't know: He came to me for support while moving through a tumultuous separation. As he presented with pain, I listened to his body talk, rather than encouraging more storytelling. I knew the questions he needed answered were within him. I knew once he released the unexpressed anger, the space left within him would be clear. How did I know this? It's become my experience every time I work with folks, and every time I do my own release work.

When he was finished, he sat down and took a drink of water.

"Her reactions aren't about me," he said simply.

He spoke these words like a Guru sitting cross legged on a mountain. His *people pleaser* robe had been removed, and replaced with a Captain's hat as he was now setting sail, mapping out his own course. As I walked him out, he said he felt lighter and exhausted, with a hint of elation.

The next morning he texted me, "My shoulder and knee pain are completely gone!"

I'm not sure which one of us was more excited!

Anger is a healthy emotion when expressed in a way that does not harm anyone or anything else, including ourselves. Releasing anger in a healthy way, and with support affords the body a feeling of relief and revitalization! Releasing the unexpressed emotion offers a feeling of lightness, and clarity, making the ability to make decisions easier once the anger has been moved. I invite you to take moments as you read through to explore what your internal dialogue tells you when you are angry, and what you should do with your feelings. Be kind to you as you take this exploration. The messaging you have currently has brought you here. Breathe as you determine what adjustments you might wish to make moving forward.

"And to heal, you must first allow yourself to feel everything."

/ZAHRA

CHAPTER 12: FOLLOW THE YELLOW BRICK ROAD

Religion was confusing to me growing up. Knowing a symptom of fear to be confusion, it makes sense that I felt unsure about what having faith, or being *faithful* meant. I was taught that Christians didn't lie or steal, and they went to church on Sundays. I grew up thinking that being a Christian meant being *superior* to those that weren't. Yet behind closed doors, I was treated as less than human, at times. You couldn't speak up if you didn't agree, or ever use the word *hate*, but you *could* rob your child or wife of their safety and dignity by hitting or shaming them. That didn't seem right. It was okay if you sent your kids to church on Sunday while you stayed home and slept. And going to church on Sundays might mean *just* the Sundays that fall on holidays like Mother's Day. The Commandments told me to honour my father, and also told me that man was created in God's image. If this behavior mirrored God, I didn't think I wanted much to do with Him. If a commandment named 'self abandonment' was a sin, then I was headed straight for hell from birth anyway.

I remember moments in church, especially during the singing of hymns, feeling a sense of warmth within my chest. To this day, I still experience a feeling of comfort when a church organ is playing. This visceral response tells me my body remembers some comforting experiences in church as a child. We went to my Nanny's United church (my mother's mom) on Mother's Day, every year. It was the same church my mom, sister and I attended when we were little, after my mom and biological father separated. I loved going there because we always went to my Nanny's afterwards, where she would make pancakes from scratch. She let me pile the butter and syrup on them, and I took full advantage of that! To this day, pancakes with syrup is my favourite meal. My belly felt settled when I ate there.

From time to time, I went to a Baptist church on a pool liner blue bus that picked me up from my house. My mom and step-dad didn't go, but I would see my Nana, my step-father's mom, there. Each time I got off the bus, the driver would hold out a Laura Secord sucker. He would hold it in his hand and only release it to me when I promised I would return the following Sunday. With a flood of anxiety, I would agree to come the next week and be rewarded with the sucker.

I was *saved* at the Baptist church. I didn't really know what that meant, but I remember the tenderness and warmth coming from my Nana's face when she watched me stand up to invite Jesus Christ into my heart. I remember feeling chosen; not by Jesus, but by my Nana. I didn't understand what was said, and the only bible verses I knew well were the ones I had memorized for Sunday school. At the time, it was fear of getting into trouble, not a desire to learn about God and religion that had me learning bible stories. I wanted to be *saved* because my Nana was always so incredibly kind and loving to me. She never asked me for anything. I wanted to make her smile; and she did.

Though I hardly attend church as an adult, I have a growing spiritual awareness and strength today. I've released the rigidity that shaped my perception of religion. I have found a sense of freedom and connection. It exists beyond the confines of any one *named* religion; I found faith. And it's faith that has the ability to heal. For me, the *proof* that a God, Mother Earth, Buddha, or Spirit presence exists, is my life experience. The story I was given shouldn't see me here preparing to share nuggets of my healing journey and how I reclaimed myself. Logic sees me living a life of pain, fear, and self abandonment with no hope of a different path. My desire to heal my pain has come from something I can only describe as inner knowing. I call this wisdom my faith. Most of my experiences of church and religion have been about not getting into trouble, or pleasing the adults in my life. When I made the decision to challenge the story I had been given as a child, I quickly learned that having an openness to spirituality and faith would be essential in my process.

I needed *trust* to take my voyage to healing. I had no idea what that looked or felt like, but I knew I needed it. I didn't have it with anyone, including myself; yet. It's interesting to me to look back at how hard I tried to control my belief in a higher power. If I could please my Nana by walking up the aisle in church and asking to be saved, would that also qualify me to be a good Christian? If I could get on the blue bus every Sunday, memorize the Bible verses, and win a bouquet of Laura Secord suckers, would I be a good Christian? If I could *watch my language*, watch the *right* shows, listen to the *right* music, was I a good Christian?

What makes sense to me today, is the *removal* of roles, of armour, of scanning the room to see what folks *need* me to be through a lense of fear and control, which allows me the freedom to show up as myself!

I found my faith by checking-in with myself. It's been there all along. Like Dorothy in The Wizard of Oz; searching for the Emerald City that held her answers, she had them with her all along. If I am created in the image of God, learning to trust myself means I no longer need to check-in with the world around me for value or approval. I can trust in the image I am created from. My yellow brick road, my spiritual path leads to my essence. I can trust in myself.

"A gut feeling is actually every cell in your body making a decision."

DEEPAK CHOPRA

CHAPTER 13: THE PAIN OF SHAME

I remember realizing, perhaps for the first time, how scared I was as a parent. I was a counsellor at a women's shelter, and a part-time personal trainer at a college gym. I was 8 years into my relationship with my second, and current husband. I brought my three children from my previous marriage, and my husband and I had two more kids together. My biological father had just died, and my oldest daughter was 15. She had reached the same age I was when I first left home. I didn't recognize the parallel at the time.

l had given Madison, my eldest, *the smile.*

I tried so hard to take it back when I saw it. She had a boyfriend and suddenly every decision revolved around this new relationship. I find it fascinating how clearly *I* saw the decisions she was making came from a place of wanting to be loved. *I* could see the glasses she wore when she looked in the mirror. She saw *only* flaws in her reflection. It was easy for *me* to name the untruths she was telling herself, yet I remained oblivious of my own. The one-time tie-wearing, Avril Lavigne singing, creative crafter, camp loving and open hearted young girl seemed to slip away before my eyes. I believed then, my job was to save her. I believed that was *my* job because I felt *I* was responsible for her suffering. It was easy to take the blame. *She* didn't choose her parents, *I* did. *She* didn't choose a mom lacking self-worth and awareness. That is what she got though. She didn't *choose* to be raised as a child of an alcoholic. She didn't choose what she witnessed behind closed doors.

Of course I told her she was brilliant, beautiful and capable. I told all five of my children this from birth. I put them in recreational and competitive sports, dance, drama, jiu jitsu, horseback riding, swimming, volleyball, day and overnight camps, all starting at the age of three. I put them in anything and everything, hoping to boost self-confidence, awareness, strength and courage. If only I had focussed as much on building *my own* confidence and self-awareness. Back then I wanted to master the role of being a mother. Looking back, I was fuelled by guilt and shame. I knew the lessons that came from witnessing an abusive relationship in the family home. I learned them well.

The feelings of guilt and shame continued to build as the conflicts with my first-born continued in the home. They consumed me. I felt frozen in fear and shame. I could see how my children were hurting, and I felt it was all my fault.

I kept true to my experience of *what happened behind closed doors, stayed behind closed doors* for quite awhile. No one at work knew. None of my friends knew. I even kept what was happening from my sister. I should have known better. I knew the impact of growing up with abuse and addiction; yet here I was, gifting the same cloak of shame and guilt to my children. Each of them struggled, and I know I did the best I could with what I knew back then. Like members of the Royal Family, they were following in their Royal birth lineage; without a choice. The crown *l* was passing on would offer the riches of pain and misery. I know now, it would also offer resilience, courage, strength, tenacity and a loving heart.

I remember having a quick conversation with a gym member who had just retired from over 20 years as a principal at a high school. He noticed I wasn't smiling, and approached me as if he knew my struggles. He started telling me he'd had hundreds and hundreds of conversations with parents in his office who were convinced their kids were on the wrong path. Their kids had joined a group of kids doing drugs or smoking; he called them the *smokers 'n tokers*.

He said, "Danielle, often the difference between the group of smokers 'n tokers and a football team is membership."

I said, "What do you mean?"

He continued, "A football team allows maybe 40 players, a soccer team, possibly 20, and a volleyball team, even less."

At this point he got off his bike, and leaned-in closer to me.

"Even club memberships are determined by specific interests or skills. But, the smokers 'n tokers have unlimited membership! Anyone can join, and everyone is welcome."

He said this was one of the biggest takeaways for him in his thirty-plus years of experience with youth in the school system.

Truth be told, this story provided temporary relief for me. I was grateful for the minute it gave me; imagining my daughter's sudden change in behavior was just a phase. Somehow I knew otherwise, but it felt good to pretend. For a minute, I believed that Madison would learn to choose herself. For a minute, I believed this chapter would be short-lived. For a minute. I believed I wasn't losing her to an eating disorder and addiction. It was a minute of bliss.

Even though her story would take her more than a minute to write, had I been driven by trust rather than fear and control back then, I could have made better use of the brilliant story I'd been told. I think he was telling me that my daughter just wanted to belong. I think he wanted me to realize that I didn't have any control over the group my daughter chose to fit into. The only control I had was how I took care of myself, and I think he was encouraging me to do so. I just couldn't hear him then. I'm so grateful that I can hear him now.

I felt completely out of control. At the time, I seemed to have pieces of myself scattered everywhere. My biological father had died suddenly. I felt robbed of a chance for reconciliation and healing with him. Back then, I didn't know the space for deep healing that was waiting for me. I didn't know this pressure cooker of fear and grief I embodied was about to blow, and this explosion would be a pivotal moment in my life. It was like a dormant volcano erupted without warning, and despite my athleticism, the lava was quickly reaching my heels. Madison was actually helping me embark on the journey back to myself, though I didn't know it at the time. This would prove to be the only mutually beneficial road. I had no control over her pain. I could own my role in it, but the responsibility for healing her wounds was hers. Drowning in shame and blame was like a slow death for me, and did nothing for any of my children. I could blame my parents for the painful life lessons, but the responsibility to heal and remove the barriers I'd placed between myself, love, and connection was mine alone. The same was true for my daughter.

The short poem below was written by a brilliant friend with whom I've done some group work. It helped me through years of witnessing womens' trauma stories, and especially when my own children struggled. The words were so powerful to me, I had them tattooed on my arm.

They are Suffering
They are Held
I will witness
I will Love Myself

I was unaware of the role shame and guilt played in my parenting until many years after all five of my children were born. My greatest lesson Ive learned is to focus on healing the painful story I had been telling myself about who I was, rather than trying to fix the mistakes I thought I had and was making with my children. I had to recognize the only person I could heal was myself, and that my personal work would impact them.

"We cannot shame ourselves in to change. We can only love ourselves in to evolution."

UNKNOWN

CHAPTER 14: THE LINE UP

I was introduced to Susan Aaron and *Psychodramatic Bodywork*® in my late thirties. My co-worker Norma suggested I attend a three-day Introductory workshop. Truth be told, I dodged Norma for over twelve years because she scared me. She seemed so *grounded,* and *connected*. It was as if she could *see* me; behind my smile, my roles, my control and my fear. She saw what I couldn't see yet; my worth and my courage. She seemed to know who I was before my painful story made me lose myself. She was leading me toward the tools that would help me remember. I was like a lost ship in the fog. Norma was my lighthouse.

I'd been watching Norma use unique techniques to support women who had experienced intimate partner abuse. I had no doubt the work was powerful. I'd witnessed some immediate mindset shifts for women, and coworkers alike. What made me uncomfortable wasn't the outcome of this therapeutic modality, but the training required to use it. As a trauma-informed counsellor, I was passionate about supporting women in *their* healing. Learning these skills would mean turning the mirror I held up for women, *on myself.*

Being around Norma felt very foreign to me. I didn't understand why, and not knowing was scary. I planned to avoid her and this workshop. She would encourage me to slow down, sometimes just by taking a deep breath herself. She'd seen me over the years with multiple sports injuries, and several surgeries. Norma talked about feelings; *a lot*. She spoke with a gentle authority that rocked me *like a babe in arms*. She always greeted me like she'd been waiting for me. She listened with her ears and heart open. She spoke with the *knowing* of a Shaman, and radiated with a wise innocence.

Norma said this training talked about where we held emotions in our bodies, and how to safely release them. She talked about the healing opportunities for myself and the folks I worked with. She said this modality was group work, and a shift from *talking* about the scary stories, to *releasing* the emotions that were suppressed at the time the trauma occurred. She said it would be time to do *my own* work. *That's* what made me uncomfortable. Here I was, *a counselor*, scared to do *my own* healing work!

When I found the strength to attend courses in Bodywork, I wanted to participate in only two ways. I wanted to listen, or talk. When I talked, I wanted to talk fast. I wanted to talk at the speed of an airplane taking off from a runway.

If I talked quickly enough, I wouldn't *feel* anything.

If I spoke fast, I could include every detail of my trauma to validate my fear to the group.

I unconsciously minimized *my* experiences of trauma. I thought I needed to share every detail. I was *sure* the group would think I was weak for being so scared. I *needed* them to know the details. I didn't want to share, but when I did, I over-shared, often void of emotion; even stoic. My heart would race, but no one knew. I hoped my titanium shell was successfully masking my trembling insides. Perhaps my need for control and to hide fear was helpful in the beginning of my personal work. Had it not been for my drive to appear fearless and in control, I'd have run away at the first sign of my sweaty armpits!

Bodywork was going to challenge my role as the *master controller of my emotions, and* my body, including my heart. I believed the fewer people I let into my heart, the safer I'd be. It's always been about control. The truth is I have to honour that perhaps the greatest role I created, the one role that ruled my kingdom of roles, was the mirror of who I saw my fathers to be: *Controllers.*

Being controlling meant being untrusting and stuck! I began a shift in my self awareness from the moment I stepped into that circle at my first training. It took courage to get there. I was already committed to personal growth when I arrived.

But this was different. I had my bathing cap on. I was diving in. Choosing to step-in was like removing the feed and the runoff from my pond, and allowing the healthy flow of emotions to resume in my body. I pictured my body like an electrical cord with nine tight knots. I had a clear understanding of the impact these knots played in controlling the flow of energy within my body. The knots controlled my ability to receive and release energy. More importantly, I saw these knots for the first time as *temporary.*

The role of counselor was safe for me. I got to support women and hold space for their scary stories; it wasn't about me, and I didn't want it to be. I finally agreed to go to the workshop because another co-worker signed up too. I decided I was going to learn additional tools in order to better my abilities as a counselor. I was going to leave my own story tucked safely inside my protective shell. Looking back at this particular time in my life, I realize I was sinking.

I didn't want to go because I was scared. But I wanted to go because I wanted to take the keys from my fear. I knew fear had been driving the bus for far too long.

I wondered, *"What if this course was a way out for me? A way out of the confines of the titanium shell I'd crafted and been hiding in? Or more so a way into me?"*

Was it possible to reach within myself and trust that the hand of my essence was there to grab hold? Did I have the strength, courage and care enough for *myself* to do *my own* work? I knew that I held a lot of blame, shame and guilt. Facing my own darkness scared me. *Feeling* my own darkness terrified me. At that time, I truly felt shackled to the story I was given. I didn't believe I had a choice to move out of my trauma home. My coworker, and dear friend, saw my ability to move with great clarity.

I wonder if she saw me like a circus elephant tied by a tiny string; held back only by the belief that I couldn't break free?

The first two days of this three-day course, I did nothing. Well, that's not entirely accurate. I smiled. I said, "Thank you" and, "No thank you", with a smile to every assisting team member that approached me.

It's hard to articulate just how scared I was those first two days. In trauma, our body shifts gears to *fight, flight, freeze* or *fawn*. *Fawning* is like a child in an abusive home, or the partner in an abusive marriage who does anything the abuser wants in order to stay safe. I was moving back and forth between freezing and fawning. I was disconnected from my body because I was so scared. I could barely hear what was being said, and if my legs weren't so jittery with fear, I might have run!

I was excited to implement what I was learning when I returned to work. But my terror took over when Susan and her team organized participants into groups to put into practice what we were learning. There I stood, halfway through day one of a three-day workshop, where I was learning about the negative impact on our organs when emotions are suppressed.

"How can I learn these therapeutic techniques without releasing any emotion?"

This is the thought that raced through my mind at lightning speed. It was like I was rapidly flipping the pages of resumes in my mind. "There must be an adequately armoured role I can step-in to survive this workshop!" I was panicking.

I spent the next day and a half witnessing what I would *now* call "absolutely beautiful." Back then, I would describe what I witnessed as "something from *The Twilight Zone*." One by one, members of our group were sharing their feelings, being supported by a hand on the back or even a hug. I remember watching, and thinking how different our world would be if folks could find safe spaces and people to share their feelings with. I just wanted to run away.

So I did the only thing I knew how to do: I smiled. And kept my vulnerability hidden. "Phew, I've found a role to hide in."

I think I felt pretty confident, initially, that my smile was a master disguise, sure to fool everyone. I believed I had the smile that would impress Secret Agent 007 himself!

By the end of day two, I felt certain I had wasted the money and was destined to live my life in a complete facade, behind my smile, with fear driving the bus. I *wanted* to be free; I really did.

I was witnessing the relief on the faces of this phenomenal group, and the space we were in seemed to be expanding around me. I became increasingly aware of the tightening sensations occuring *within* me. It was as if my *armored smile* was beginning to suffocate me like a boa constrictor. Looking back though, had I known how hard day three of training was going to be, I would have remained the wallflower I was for the first two days; or I'd have left. I would have packed up my bags of fear, and driven home; facade intact. But as I would soon discover, *Psychodramatic Bodywork*® offered me the chance to explore the self behind my smile. What a discovery that would await me!

Day three of the workshop was my walk through the guarded gates of the sphinxes, except there were no mythical creatures shooting lasers at me when I showed my fear. Of course, my years of conditioning had me feeling certain there might be.

It would instead see me facing the nine men in my life who had abused me. These nine men taught me how to lower my worth, hurt myself, run, and shut down. They collectively birthed my need to create an unbreachable fortress that held my fear and grief in.

Day three showed me that fear and grief were not alone in my fortress. On the contrary: One by one, I'd brought-in each of the nine men and the painful beliefs they gave me, right into my fortress! Seeing this was scary. *Feeling* this seemed impossible, but somehow I just knew this was the work I was called to do. I don't know how or why I trusted, but I did. I had to *feel* how much space they took up in my body, and flush them out. This would be a spring cleaning I'd never forget. It would soon be time to pack up their beliefs, and move them all out!

I walked into day three and took my place in the circle. There were over twenty of us attending the workshop. There were registered participants like myself, and many assistants carefully selected by Susan to offer support when needed. I was familiar with sitting in circles with groups as this is how we lead groups with women in my workplace. There is a *rigidity* that is removed from a space when a circle is created. Susan explained that today was the day a psychodrama would take place. Working closely with my co-worker Norma, and Desi, who also attended, I was somewhat familiar with witnessing, even providing some support during a small psychodrama for clients.

Before I explain what happened next, I'd like to examine why group work is so powerful in shifting core beliefs.

Group work offers a healing experience by virtue of being in a group and being safe. This is in sharp juxtaposition to the first group in which most people belong: their families. This is particularly true if those family settings are unsafe. This is what makes group work so powerful.

Everyone has messages from their family of origin that are both helpful and harmful. Parts of our *childhood emotional body* are bound to be awakened any time we step into a group setting. A dinner with friends, the workplace, a fitness class; these are all opportunities for the helpful and harmful messages and beliefs we once heard and felt in our families of origin to arise. The greater our self-awareness of what these messages are, and whether they are hurtful or helpful, the more the stage is set for connections, as we experience a sense of belonging in these groups. Group settings are opportunities for new relationships to bloom and existing ones to be nurtured. At the same time, a lack of awareness can see group settings as a place to prove the harmful childhood beliefs to be true.

In my own experience, if I felt I was not seen or heard as a child in my family of origin, I could always walk-in to any group setting and search for proof that I was (and am), in fact, *not seen or heard*. This would be especially possible if I had not dedicated space and time to gaining self-awareness. I may only see the people who don't greet me, and ignore those who do. I may step back from conversation, rather than stepping-in for connection. It's possible that I might play a role in keeping the painful childhood story of *"I'm not seen or heard,"* alive.

Back to our story...

Susan sat with graceful intention. Her face was framed with flowing white curls, and her eyes blanketed us all with warmth at every glance. Her voice was strong and sweet, like a specialty coffee with a shot of vanilla. She embodied the kindness of my Irish Nana, and exuded confidence in providing direction and movements like my Nanny did. Her husband Paul was partnered beside her. He stood *conveniently* over 6 feet in height like my husband Jeff. His height took-up space, yet his demeanor was accepting of what was to come.

Susan addressed the group, "Does anyone have a piece of work they would like to present in a psychodrama today? If you do, please step into the circle. Once you've stepped-in, think about how you'll explain your work to the group. From there, the group will choose by placing a hand on the person they *feel* has a piece of work that resonates most with them. Through a process of elimination, the person with the most hands on them will be chosen, and the psychodrama will begin."

The room was quiet when Susan finished her instructions. I'm not sure if folks were looking around the room or at each other. My eyes were fixated on the floor in front of me.

"Did I have a piece of work?" I posed the question to myself. The churning in my stomach announced that I did.

The next thing I knew, I had stepped forward. To this day, I'm not sure how I did because my legs felt like they were filled with concrete. My stomach instantly doubled as a butterfly sanctuary. My face was flushed and I'd already begun to sweat.

"I haven't even said anything yet!" I thought to myself. "What was I even *going* to say?"

Susan gave a *last call* to anyone wanting to present a piece of work. The room was quiet. The others that stepped in the circle, like me, seemed nervous. Susan made her way from person to person asking that we share with the group our desired piece of work. I still don't remember what anybody else said. I remember feeling crowded. The process of elimination saw me standing in the middle of the circle, surrounded by the group, having chosen *my* piece. I do remember her honouring each person whose drama had *not* been chosen.

Susan approached me, and must have known I was terrified. She was slow and kind when offering me direction. I'm sure I appeared like a deer in headlights. She first asked that I choose a support person to stand with me. I chose Norma. Norma placed her hand on my back. It would be over two hours before she would remove it.

I had no idea how to answer Susan's question: "What was my piece of work?"

I heard myself say, "I want to have a good relationship with my husband." That's all I said.

"What does that even mean?" I thought to myself.

What Susan did next was walk through a series of questions that she *intuitively* put together. I know they came from a place of intuition, as we processed the psychodrama afterwards.

Processing is when questions are posed to the director (Susan) about the *hows* and *whys* of the drama. The question and answer sessions are how the group learns the therapeutic techniques of a psychodrama.

I don't remember what she asked me. But I do recall having to ask her to repeat her questions. My legs were shaking. I was so grateful for Norma's support at my back. Despite my fear, I knew if I collapsed, she would catch me.

Susan quickly concluded that fear and trust were core issues for me. Her questions led to asking where trust had been broken in my life. I began naming the men in my life who had hurt me, beginning with my biological father. Each time I gave a name,

I was instructed to choose a member of the group to *play the role* of that individual.

"What do you mean?" I couldn't believe she was asking me to make that kind of selection.

How could she ask me to pick someone to play the role of a physically, emotionally, or sexually abusive man? I didn't understand why she had me do this, but *something* in me trusted her. I was trusting in this process and in Susan's integrity and wisdom. I'd only known Susan for two days, but through Norma, I'd known her for ten years.

I sat scanning the group of people I had met just two days prior. One by one, I selected someone to play the role of an abuser in my life. I couldn't believe what I was seeing when my list was complete. There were eight individuals standing in a line in front of me. It was amazing how I felt looking at their faces. They looked *nothing* like the eight men who had abused me, but it *felt* like they were.

My heart was racing, and I could feel a sweat droplet slide down my spine. *It was sure to be the first of many,* I thought to myself. Then she asked me to pick someone to play Jeff, my husband.

She stood the eight individuals in a row, and had the person playing Jeff stand behind them. I instantly saw and *felt* why I struggled to *see* my husband! There were eight abusers, and the painful stories they'd given me, between us.

I did everything in that moment to hold back the tears. I was overcome with nausea. I thought it was going to throw up. The sweat was rolling down my back and my front by this time. I wanted to run. My legs were shaking, yet I felt frozen. I was terrified.

I turned to Susan, and heard myself say, "I don't know what's happening. I feel sick."

With Norma's hand still firmly placed on my back, Susan offered me permission to have my feelings.

I remember saying, "I don't know what to do."

I now know I was flooded with many of the symptoms of unexpressed fear. I recall locking eyes with a member of the group who was still sitting. She was crying. *"Why was she crying?"* I thought to myself.

Susan then asked me a question that forced me to give my feelings a voice. She asked me to look at the first man, and tell him what *line* he gave me. I didn't know what she meant at first.

"What line?" I asked her.

She directed me to *feel* the energy of that abuser, and then check *within myself* for the *message* I took from how he treated me. I still felt confused by her direction. My legs shook more and my nausea grew. Susan asked me to share something about the first man who hurt me, my biological father. It's interesting that I put him first in the line-up, in spite of the fact that I'd told the group about trauma in my teenage years.

Once upon a time, I'd gone to stay with him for a week. I wanted to prove he wasn't as scary as I'd been told. I had very little contact with him between the ages of five and fourteen;

the odd letter, postcard or gift. After his years as a police officer, he worked as a mercenary. *Yes, you read that correctly.* This meant postcards came from places like El Salvador. I remember taking one to school for show and tell. I can't help but wonder what the teacher must have thought. I wanted to prove to my mom and stepfather that he wasn't *as bad* as they said he was.

Instead, he proved to be as bad as they said. My week turned into just one night. I hitchhiked to a friend's house at 3am after surviving what felt like a nightmare. My dad got drunk. He exposed himself to me by urinating outside my car window. He yelled profanities at me in the stands of a crowded hockey game. He chased me down the street in a drunken rage. He nearly broke the jaw of one of his tenants who had jumped-in to protect me. He didn't know I took off until he woke up the next day.

I don't imagine there would have been much recognition or ownership of the night before anyway. Fortunately, *or unfortunately,* I was seasoned with witnessing, or being at the receiving end of, a drunk man's violence. The absence of an apology, recognition of the trauma, or ownership for the behaviour was *normal to me.* One of the things I believed, being a child of an alcoholic, was that I wasn't good enough to be chosen. If I were, spending time with *just me,* without the bottle of dark rum, would have been *enough* for my Dad.

Sharing this experience with Susan and the group helped me feel a bit more *connected* to the *feelings* I felt that night in the hockey arena, and running down the street. When I shared this experience with someone before, I felt nothing. What I understand now, and perhaps what I was coming to terms with in this moment of the psychodrama, was all my feelings connected to that trauma remained *unexpressed* in my body all these years.

> *"Trauma is not what happens to you, it's what happens inside you as a result of what happened to you. Trauma is that scarring that makes you less flexible, more rigid, less feeling and more defended." Dr Gabor Mate*

One by one, I gave each chosen individual their *line*. I solidified the presentation of their role by draping a scarf around each person's neck. I walked over to a pile, chose a scarf, then placed it on the person playing my dad and said, "You're not good enough." My voice seemed to echo in the hollows of my titanium shell.

"Eat it or wear it." That was the next one.

"You're only good for one thing."

The traumatic experience with my dad took the most time to tell. As I moved down the line of abusers, the stories shortened. I said less, and felt more. My legs shook more, and sweat was starting to show through my clothing.

"You don't matter."

"You're a slut."

"You're worthless."

"You're not deserving of being loved."

"Your needs and feelings don't matter."

When the last person said their line, I stood staring blankly at Susan. I was freezing, and was visibly shivering.

"I can't feel anything." I told Susan.

Susan's next direction revealed her twenty plus years of experience in Psychodramatic Bodywork®. She directed the group to walk over to me, remove their scarves, and place them around *my* neck while stating their line to me.

One by one, the line up of eight gave me their scarves and their lines. I stood there staring blankly. Susan then directed the group of eight to yell their lines at me all at once. I stood there, wearing the eight scarves and started to feel the rocks hitting my barricade. I tried desperately to hold back my tears. Suddenly my titanium shell seemed to transform into glass. The volume of the messages increased. The shrill pitch of the eight voices shattered my casing. The pieces of my *grand facade* lay scattered at my feet.

I met eyes once again with the crying woman I'd spied before. This time I couldn't see her clearly as tears were streaming down my face too. I realize she helped me feel safe enough to cry. She helped validate my traumatic story. Her tears showed me that what I'd endured, the abuse I survived, *was* scary. This woman, I just met, was having *her* sadness witnessing *my* trauma. She helped give me *permission* to *feel* something for *myself.*

I looked back at Susan and she told me, though she didn't speak. "There's no rush." I *felt* her just *witnessing* me in my pain, and letting me have my process. It's as if she *knew* me, or many others *like* me. She was holding me unconditionally. I was sandwiched between two slices of unconditional love. Norma at my back, and Susan standing in front of me facilitating this deeply painful and powerful drama that would change the lens through which I viewed the world moving forward. I looked around the room where I stood, and there wasn't a dry eye. There were so many tears. I felt as if I were bathing in the grief of thousands of traumas. Remembering the group of over twenty people I attended this training with, I'm certain I was.

Before dismissing my abusers, Susan had me, one by one, return the scarves and the messages. The line up of eight left the *stage*. I wasn't left alone though. I had Norma at my back, Susan still directing, and *Jeff* who had been standing behind the line up of eight the entire time. I was asked to give him a line.

The line that came to me was simply, "I'm here."

That's all that came out. I felt a weight lifted from my chest as I spoke those two simple words. I stood staring at him, not knowing what to do. Susan asked if I wanted a hug. I did, but was still afraid to ask. The person in the role of Jeff walked over and hugged me. I knew at that moment I had my work cut out for me. I say this because I *tried* to say yes to the hug, but couldn't speak. I just *couldn't*. I felt the need to speak, within me, but it was deep in the hollows of my shell, still anchored in shame. Healthy intimacy had been hard for me, but this experience gave me hope that it was possible.

If I could learn to receive love, I could learn to ask for it too. Perhaps nothing was wrong with me like I'd assumed my whole life. Trauma *happened* to me, but it did not have to define me. The seed of truth was planted that day.

Susan asked me if I needed anyone else to come on the stage. "No thank you." She asked where my mother was. I drew a blank. I followed her instructions to pick someone to be my mom, and I gave her a scarf. I couldn't think of a *line* to give her. Susan told me that was ok, but she felt my mom should have a place on stage. I looked at her, and felt blank.

I now understand that I was feeling my mother's *absence* in my life. My mom was there my whole life, but she was very busy navigating her own trauma for much of it. I have always known my mom loves me.

This part of the drama was healing because I held so much guilt for my own absence in my children's lives. This piece helped me be kinder to myself, just as I had always held kindness for my mom and her lived experience of abuse.

It was powerfully raw, and undeniably validating and healing for me. There was nothing wrong with me. I had survived trauma, but I was not the cause of the trauma, nor did it have to define me. These few paragraphs don't do my psychodrama justice. It was a significant piece of personal work that will stay with me forever. It was nine years ago, and I still continue to uncover new nuggets of learning from it. I'm forever grateful for the lessons that reminded me of who I am; who I've *always* been.

"Pay attention to your patterns. The way you learned to survive may not be the way you want to live. Heal and shift."

DR ATHENA BRYANT

CHAPTER 15: A TURTLE'S PACE

I am *healing.* I've often equated the speed at which I learn and heal to that of a turtle. I *used* to say it to put myself down, or *make fun* of myself for being such a slow learner.

I'd say, "I was a kid that needed to burn my hand on the hot stove several times before I understood *not* to touch it!"

Little jokes? *Perhaps.* The underlying tone was that I *believed* something was wrong with me. I *believed* I wasn't good enough. I believed I should hide in my shell. I believed my soft, emotional vulnerability needed to be under armoured guard. I started to believe this so deeply that I created roles that pushed my body physically and emotionally. I worked tirelessly, creating roles that hid my fear and pain of feeling *less than*. In that role, I mattered. In that role, I was of value. I pushed myself to such an extent that I was manifesting the story I believed. Covered in stitched wounds, surgical scars, and a closet full of crutches and medical braces, I was becoming the picture of brokenness I had worked so hard to disguise.

> *"Personality is nothing more than a structure you have built to keep yourself from being hurt."* Dr Gabor Mate, *When the Body Says No.*

I am *healing.* I still greatly admire the turtle, though my relation to it has morphed to better fit my essence. I see the movement of the turtle, a sea turtle especially, as majestic and intentional. They appear to move at a pace that suits *their* purpose. Even their faces seem to wear smiles of satisfaction; an expression worn when peace has been pulled out from the inside. The removal of 'roles' means opening the door to infinite possibilities, infinite thoughts and experiences. I am. Well, I just AM. Without roles, my essence exists *without* borders! I'm free to ebb and flow with the current, in spaces that feel right for *me*. **TRUST in self now exists, rather than trust in roles.** I have stepped out of my titanium shell and let the guilt and shame I've been carrying drop.

Shame is defined by Brene Brown as, *"an intensely painful feeling or experience of believing that we are flawed and therefore unworthy of love and belonging."*

The exercise of returning the scarves that held the false truths in my Psychodrama, was a pivotal moment in my life. It was like cracking open a concrete tomb to unleash the *untruths* of my existence. The false lens through which I had been seeing the world, and most importantly, seeing myself, was removed. Perhaps similar to the blinding sensation when sunglasses are removed in the bright sun, my vision of self has taken time to adjust to the light of my own reflection. I'm learning to allow myself the same grace I give to others when they are learning a new skill.

Like building a bicep muscle, it takes time and consistency to embrace the truth of who I was before I took ownership of the messages from the abusers in my life.

After seven years of learning from Susan Aaron, I graduated from her Advanced Training Program in 2020. I continue attending Group Training biannually with Susan. My group members fly across the province, drive, and fly-in from New York to meet and do this unique deep healing work together. It's so incredibly powerful in its simplicity. Tell your story until you connect with the feeling. Interrupt the common practice of suppressing the emotion to complete the storytelling. Name the feeling that comes up for you. And with practice, naming the feeling comes with ease, then you are able to release it!

Psychodramatic Bodywork® had me playing out conversations with men that had abused me in my life. I felt the fear, the sadness, the deep unexpressed anger that I was unable to express at the time I experienced the trauma.

Dialogue plays a part in psychodrama. It helps give the protagonist, and the rest of the group context. The deepest part of the healing is in recognizing the unexpressed emotion, and being able to safely release it. This allows healing, and the ability to move forward. The scary story still exists, but the level of fear doesn't. Therefore, when scary things or things that make me angry or sad happen; instead of that igniting all of the unexpressed feelings connected to the past trauma, I'm able to respond to the present day experience or event. I can be clear in feeling and releasing the emotions that come up. My body suffers less physically, emotionally, mentally, and spiritually. Many folks come to this work who are therapists or have experienced trauma and want to heal. **I came to this work to be a better counselor, and have instead become my truer healing self!**

Adults in society are not given free rein to scream. We've given all the permission for spontaneous emotional releases to the kids! We have created *socially acceptable* platforms for adults, like the roller coaster at an amusement park, a bungy jump, or the snow tubing hill at a ski resort. They all provide an abundance of terror for our *fear releasing* pleasure!

What if you don't like scary rides or extreme sports? If a scream can relieve suppressed fear held in the body, a scream into a pillow, or uninhibited release while seated with a trained support *can* be just as effective. We let our feelings out more freely as children, but it's a skill that *can* be relearned as adults with support and practice.

One of my favourite fear release practices to do with individuals and groups is to walk on a forest trail. A vigorous walk helps to increase the heart rate and the expansion of the lungs, creating an open window for grief. The digging-in of the heels during a good sandy hill climb can help loosen the body's grip on anger too, and this is my window to encourage sound from deep in the belly to let that out. Reaching the top of the hill often sees the door to unexpressed fear swing open, which allows the holder to let some of it out with a victorious scream.

No sooner had I written the previous paragraph than I received a phone call from a woman I've worked with off and on for years. She is brilliant and resilient in navigating her life through unimaginable trauma. She called to thank me. She was having feelings, and stepped into her old familiar pattern of holding them in, and dove into distraction. But! She interrupted herself!

She said, "I know that worked before, but it doesn't feel right anymore."

Do you know what she shared next? She went straight outside to the hill outside her residence, and did somersaults!

She said, "I knew I just needed to shake it out somehow, and I asked myself what my little self wanted to do? Next thing I knew, I was outside rolling on the lawn, laughing and winded!" Her voice sang with excitement, "I'm so proud of myself, Danielle!"

My heart sang opera when she shared this with me. I thanked her for trusting herself to work with me, and for doing the work which was in turn deepening my trust for myself! She had experienced symptoms of unexpressed fear, tried old behaviours, became aware of her reactions, and decided to honour her body by releasing the fear with an incredible, simplistic yet empowering action! Who knew somersaults could be so healing?!

Watching movies or television shows can also be a great way to release unexpressed emotion. At the end of a work day, I often get on the treadmill and put on Grey's Anatomy. There's sure to be a scene that will help me let out a tear or two! My body doesn't care *why* I'm letting go of grief, nor does it need me to talk about it. I just need to pay attention to the signs and symptoms of unexpressed emotion, and release them! I have been sharing this practice with folks I've supported in my role as a counselor for many years. **I encourage people to keep a list of favourite sad movies for times of grief.**

Using bodywork to release unexpressed emotion allows me to explore my creativity, and I'm able to practice on myself daily. I've learned, and continue to practice listening to my own body and the messages. I pay attention to aches and pains that I used to ignore and push through. I take advantage of fitness classes and let out a, "Woohoo!" as often as I can, conscious of the releases I'm doing. I invite the class to engage, and more and more, they are!

I love the Tony Robbins quote, *"Life happens for me, not to me."*

Going back to my beginning has shown me how I've taken what happened *to* me, and the tools I used to navigate trauma to work *for me* and to help others! This happens when I teach spin classes, and provide hill climbs with verbal instructions to connect *within* on your climb. I invite participants to connect with *themselves* physically and emotionally while raising their heart rate. I use fitness as a time for mind/body connection with both increased and decreased levels of intense exercise. I have found passion in linking the uncomfortable to the triumphs of self discovery physically, emotionally, mentally and spiritually. Making the heart busy pumping blood, and the lungs busy moving oxygen opens the doors for fluids to flow. It's not uncommon for participants to share having cried during a class. I add additional comfort and safety by turning the lights low or off for folks like me that have to work harder to access their grief.

I went for a walk with a man the other day, who is certifiably an expert in patience and vision. Full transparency here, I love the work I do! Listening to people's stories, and hearing how folks process their experiences fascinates me. I get to listen. I get to witness people sorting through vulnerable chapters of their lives. Sometimes I'm just holding space. Other moments have me validating their pain and their choices. I often feel like I'm standing with my patients as they conduct a spring cleaning in their homes. Metaphorically speaking, we walk through each room together from the bright sunroom to the dark and dingy basement. I can stand with my patients as they create the piles of what to keep, what to throw away, and even what to put into storage. In these sessions, I'm witnessing folks returning to who they were before they were given a story that told them who they weren't. I get to learn something new about myself with each conversation. The walk I was speaking about was a perfect example.

As we walked through the forest, I asked, "What do you do when you feel the need to let go of stuff?"

He was quiet for just a few steps, then responded, "I go for a walk."

This answer may not *sound* earth shattering, but what followed was nothing short of brilliant. He described what going for a walk meant to him. I listened as he listed the necessary criteria for his *release* walks:

- There can be no scheduling of the walks.
- The walk begins when his shoe hits the path.
- His desire in the moment dictates the distance.
- When he's done walking, he stops. If he's far enough from home, he calls his wife to pick him up.
- There must be changing scenery. He likes to walk up hills, down hills, through forests, and across fields alike.
- He walks slowly when he wants and speeds it up when he feels like it.
- When he feels like stopping and sitting, that's what he does.

I wondered if these *'walks without borders'* might mimic his childhood? Was this his brilliant way of reconnecting with his youth? I thought of the expression, "Youth is wasted on the young." Perhaps that's true for some. Reflecting on our conversation, I thought of the characters from the coming of age movie, *Stand By Me*. The boys in the movie came together on a quest, and left the trials of their lives behind to ban together for this *final hurrah*. The characters discuss their lives, and express fear, grief and anger throughout their quest along the railroad tracks. The adventure ends with the boys separating, one by one, acknowledging that *adulting* is on the horizon. Life as they knew it, was about to change. As the movie ends, the viewer is left with an ominous feeling of loss.

Does our ability to have fun leave us when we grow up? Unlike the movie, my walking partner is able to capture the freedom of limitless youth with each chosen adventure walk. His adventures embody the freedom of youth coupled with the choices of adulthood. Absolutely brillliant, isn't it? He absorbs every sight like a sponge sopping up a spill. The landscape is his spill. Every sound, every smell, every taste seems to beckon him.

He said, "When I walk, I feel a sense of freedom."

I watched his Chuck Taylors grip the dirt as we headed up a hill together. He continued, "I just want to see different things when I walk, and go at my own pace."

As we neared the end of our path, I examined the expression on his face. He seemed unfazed by our walk coming to an end. He remained steady with his sharing process. His blue eyes reflected the sun, and his newly pronounced rosey cheeks held a delightful glow.

The walk with my gentleman friend, and the movie, *Stand By Me*, may have appeared randomly in this book. But they're really quite intentional, and connected to what I want to share: There are very unique ways to release emotion as taught by Susan Aaron. Before doing the work myself, I thought these methods were rather strange. Laying on a gymnastics mat, acting out a full-on temper tantrum, including the screaming, in my forties, was not a therapeutic practice I was open to initially! The screaming, however, has become a necessary part of my continued fear release work. I don't have access to the mat, and the support group all the time, but I can grab a pillow with a support person on the phone. I might turn up my music in the car and bellow out a song really loudly with the consciousness that I am letting go of fear.

What relevance does this have to the walk with my friend and the movie *Stand By Me* you might be asking? What if adults practiced emotional releases using the similar brilliance we exercised as children? What I know to be true about trauma, is that the ability to be spontaneous, to trust, and to be creative is greatly diminished. The fight or flight trauma response removes the ability to connect and nurture our creativity. I wonder if this is why I became such a vivid dreamer. Similar to the main character, Will, who wrote imaginative tales that captivated his friends around the campfire, I wrote tales in my dreams. What a brilliantly safe way to explore my feelings, my imagination, and my creativity. This is a skill that I developed in trauma, and I'm delighted to share that it still exists.

My friend shared that he might spend an entire day walking. Perhaps for my friend, walking without borders is the release that works for him, and keeps him connected to the creativity and freedom of his youth.

Allow me to ask you a few questions: What did you do when you were young that made you let go and feel free? What games did you play, or adventures did you take? Did you used to dance on the lawn, or scream out to your friends playing a good game of British Bull dog? How might you incorporate what you did in your youth to help you release emotion today?

"Unexpressed emotions will never die. They are buried alive and will come forth later in uglier ways." - Sigmund Freud

I'm sharing my own body breaks with other athletes, other fitness folk, and letting people know what's working for me. I'm planting the seeds of self awareness with the gentleness, and patience that was required for me. I feel like a dandelion, trusting in the breezes that come to pass on what I've learned with the same kindness and care as was passed-on to me. I trust that my body is always speaking to me, and I respond with care and attention rather than irritation. I'm learning to slow down, and finding this new pace makes the messages more audible. I notice when I sweat because I'm scared, and I use the knowledge of this symptom as an *opportunity* to retreat into my shell, if needed, or let some fear out right away.

I'm growing increasingly intuitive; connecting to myself and to others with greater clarity. I'm learning through daily practice.

I spent some time with my dear friend Norma, not too long ago. I wanted to read to her. When I started reading, I felt like Daniel-son in the Karate Kid, sitting cross-legged in front of Sensei-Miyagi. We no longer work together in the shelter, and it's been over two years since I co-facilitated groups with Norma.

She will forever be my mentor, but as she reflected on what I'd read, and how it resonated with her, I noticed something. *I* had removed the desk between us. She was learning from me too. She shared that she had been learning from me all along. Norma never put the desk in-between us those 20 years ago when we became co-workers in the shelter; *I had*. The desk was symbolic of my shell, of the roles I had created, and played so well serving everyone, except for myself. Before we parted from our tea date together, she provided yet another valuable lesson.

She reminded me that my shell was, and continues to be brilliant. Its use has shifted from a place in which to hide, into a location similar to Superman's phone booth, where positive transformation occurs. Today, my shell is a place to retreat within myself; a place to gather my own wisdom; to reset; to slow down and take a breath; to go inward. It's my place to embrace stillness, rather than change into another role from which to run.

Stillness comes with practice, and practicing stillness is hard! It's especially difficult if you are like me, and struggle to sit still! I feel compelled to share part of a poem from Facebook,

"Living in chaos is hard, finding peace is hard; **Choose your hard.**"

I love this poem because it names three truths: Navigating fear and control in my life was exhausting. Turning the efforts I used to support others towards myself was challenging. And as an adult, I realize that I have a choice!

I have a choice to keep a childhood story alive, that no longer serves me: that I need to control my environment or I will be unsafe.

I have a choice to pull-in the support I need to heal my trauma.

I have a choice to learn how to come out from under the blanket of fear.

I can choose me. I can accept that peace resides within me.

Do you have a place you can sit and truly feel at peace? Do you have a favourite trail you walk, or spot in your backyard to which you love to retreat? Do you have a getaway destination that sees you count down the weeks each year because you are so relaxed and at ease there?

The first place I embraced *stillness was* sitting at the end of the dock, the first year I vacationed at my dear friend's cottage. Visually scanning the lake, I felt certain this place held a mystical force. I sat, watching the mist rising, then witnessed it dancing across the surface of the water. I could hear what sounded like small animals across the lake splashing at the opposite shore. I took long deep breaths. I felt so grateful for this moment, and sad knowing it would be another year before I could feel this *stillness* again. I felt the tears slide down my cheeks. My final inhalation came with the wisdom I needed. Although I can readily access this peace by the lake with my beautiful friend by my side, **the *feeling* resides within me, and can therefore be accessed anytime, and *anywhere*.**

CHAPTER 16: THE TIN MAN

I had a dream the other night that I was the Tinman in *The WIzard of OZ*. I was all made-up and in costume. I was about to step on stage, but I was no longer prepared to perform as I had been in the past. I had the costume, the metal pins and plates, but I no longer knew my lines. Although I knew I was in costume; oddly enough, I wasn't scared that I hadn't rehearsed. I felt bad for the other actors as I was certain they'd spent weeks in rehearsal, and would be mad at my unpreparedness. But instead of keeping silent, I told them about my dilemma before we went on stage. To my surprise, they told me they hadn't rehearsed either. I felt a wave of peace wash over me. It was as though I *knew* the facade had existed, but was finally over.

There are no more lines to learn. No more roles to play. I can still wear costumes; the athlete, the counselor, the mother, but scripts are no longer required. The narrative now comes from within, in real time - no script. It's like Peter Gabriel sang, *"And the grand facade, so soon will burn."* My fear had vanished, and was replaced by grief. It was a beautiful reconciled sadness that confirmed I'd had a heart all along, just like the Tinman.

My searching and running was over. *Everything I needed to know was within me.* I've always known how to love and be loved; it's a knowing that has *always* resided within me. It's a gift, given by the Divine.

In the story, Dorothy was told by the good witch, Glinda, that she had had the power to return home all along. Initially, she was confused, but then Glinda helped her look within for what she had learned, for what she knew. Like in my Intro course, I asked to have a healthy relationship with Jeff. I didn't *need* Susan, or the group or anyone to teach me *how* to love. I needed to learn how to trust. I had to trust *myself* that I was capable of receiving love. The psychodrama helped me see the story I'd created, and the roles I needed to play to fit that story.

Like the main characters in the *Wizard of Oz*, I lived in fear of not being enough to make it on my own without being taken down by my own vulnerability. In the movie, The Wicked Witch and her cast of soldiers and monkeys were lurking behind every tree, every poppy field, ready to kill Dorothy and her friends.

So let me ask you the following question: What was it that took down the wicked witch? It was water, wasn't it? I find that rather fascinating. Water; like tears from a good cry, is exactly what melted the witch. And all along, in this book, we've been examining the power inherent in releasing our emotions; crying being one of the techniques. Removing the witch made even her followers celebrate as they too were bound to her, only by fear. I didn't really need to go anywhere, as the wisdom and my feelings had been with me all along. It took until the fiftieth year of my life to come full circle, but it was a profound realization.

My dreams had and have been messages that have taken me fifty years to decipher and decode.

When I shared this dream with my husband, he said, "Maybe you feel like the Tinman because of all the hardware you have in your body from surgeries?" I thought about that. How interesting that I've had so many surgeries, and that my husband would instantly see that connection without taking a breath.

The Tin Man was the character found alone, having rusted in the rain. Dorothy oiled him up, and he joined her and the Scarecrow on the route to meet the Wizard for a new heart. Along the way, he held-in his tears, knowing something bad would happen and that his body would rust again. Luckily, any time he needed oil, his new friends were there to help him. When they finally arrive at the Emerald City, the Wizard tells him that he, in fact, had a heart all along. And he finally feels the proof of having a heart when he begins to grieve the departure of Dorothy.

When I started Psychodramatic Bodywork®, my quest was to be able to *see* my husband, and have a healthy relationship with him. I too have learned, like the tin man, that my sense of belonging needed to come from within *myself*. There was never a magic wizard I needed to find, or a role in a play that I needed to master to earn my heart; my value, or my sense of belonging. Loving myself is a journey that, like in the *Wizard of Oz*, sees me needing to look no further than my own mirror. Trauma, like the cyclone in Dorothy's dream, took me on a unique adventure where I met villains and teachers. Each encounter taught me more about my ability to navigate my own yellow brick road; my own path.

I am still learning. I think I'll be done when I die, so there's no rush! My inner narrative continues to shift and step deeper into kindness for myself. My self awareness is increasingly acute. When I am pulled into the abyss of self doubt by fear, my essence quickly scoops me up on shore to safety. My discomfort in stillness decreases with every intentional deep breath I take. When I'm at the gym, I push instead of punish; well, most of the time. When I don't listen to my body, I'm recognizing, and interrupting that old pattern more quickly and gently. Instead of jumping into blame, shame or guilt, I ask myself what my symptoms are. If I listen, they'll tell me what feeling I'm trying to suppress, when I can't figure it out. Then I release the feeling, and ask for help if I'm struggling to get to it. If I know I'm sad, even calling someone I trust can help me connect to my heart.

Funny enough, as I worked to finish this book, my knees were bothering me. So I did something I've never done: I asked for help *before* taking a dramatic fall. I also stopped jogging, and decided to simply walk on the treadmill and bike for cardio. Making that decision was hard for me. I had decided to be a runner, right after giving birth to my oldest at the age of twenty one. I realize I've always been running in fear; but at twenty one, I gave myself another official role: *the runner*. But I've taken a different kind of step this time: I called the doctor and told him my knees hurt. I stuttered and tripped over a couple of my words as I described my knee pain. He didn't call me a wimp, or tell me to suck it up. Instead, he scheduled x-rays, and MRIs before ending the call. I hung up the phone and immediately felt a pressure in my chest. I knew this symptom, yet I didn't fight it. That would only make my knee pain worse. Instead, I cried. I cried a lot. I cried for the parts of me that believed complaining about the pain was weakness. I cried in celebration for the strength I had to endure, and the courage I have now to choose a different kind of hard. Sucking it up is hard. Being gentle on my body is hard. I'm choosing the latter kind of hard.

I followed through with tests over the next six weeks. I only did a few short jogs on my treadmill during this time, and I stuck mostly to walking and biking. Just the other day, I met with the surgeon. After four surgeries on my right knee, the MRI showed it to be fully intact. The diagnosis is arthritis. I felt a lump in my chest. My left knee had a couple of issues, one of them being arthritis. The lump grew. *And* a complex tear. *I'm not going to be a runner anymore, and I'm going to need another surgery.* I thought to myself. I asked the surgeon if I could sleep on it. I decided to take a moment to breathe.

In the past I would have jumped to book the operation, without taking a breath. In the past I would have felt pissed off and embarrassed, and probably gone for a run to sweat it out. I can see that was a trauma response I adopted as a child. *'If you're scared, run!'* Trauma responses are fight, flight, freeze or fawn. I've done all four with running shoes for most of my life. I've run toward a fight, run away from myself, stood and dissociated from self, and *'fawned '*by becoming whatever I thought I needed to be in order to stay safe in a home or a relationship. The fleeing, or running, worked really well for me in the past, but my orthopedic file tells me that it won't work anymore. I've been running my whole life.

I left the appointment and walked to my car. *"Another surgery,"* I said again to myself. *"And arthritis!!" There's got to be a quick fix for this.* I felt the wave of shame building. *"Here I am, writing a book about how much I've learned to listen to my body, and I'm having another surgery resulting from overuse and pushing too hard."* *I wont play soccer or run anymore.* The shame felt nauseating. It was as if I'd eaten something I used to eat every day, and suddenly my body won't digest it. The shame wouldn't go down. It sat like a lump in my throat, and a weight on my chest. I didn't want to hold it as I had done countless times in the past. So right there in the car, I decided to do the work; to do *my* work. I cried. I cried big tears. As I cried, I didn't shame myself. I told myself I was allowed to grieve as long as I needed to. I realized I was truly grieving all of my roles that made up this Grand Facade I built to present the world; to hide myself from the world; to hide myself from myself. I cried for *little Danielle* who believed she wasn't enough. I also cried in celebration of honouring my feelings, releasing them, and moving forward without the weight of shame silencing my beautiful tears.

The personal work hasn't stopped being hard, and it won't. I'll continue to get more skilled and equipped to feel, and love myself *through* the hard. I'll forever be inspired by the courage of others working through their trauma. I grow increasingly delighted by my own ability to embrace the moment, and dance in the unknown. *Control is a Grand facade.* If I told you I was holding a cup in one hand, and control in the other, what would you be looking at? It was helpful for me to believe I held control in the past. It's come time for me to let the facade burn as it's become more harmful than helpful in my life.

I have realized something: I am complete. I always have been.

"Owning our story and loving ourselves through that process is the bravest thing we'll ever do."

BRENE BROWN

WHAT'S NEXT?!

Has reading my story got you thinking about exploring *your own* story?

For over 15 years, I've been working with people to help them through their own emotional blocks. With my own personal experiences and that of my previous clients, I'm on a mission to help others heal their own emotional blocks.

If my story resonated with you, and you'd like to discuss what working with me might look like, you can reach out to me to discuss:

- Booking a one on one with Danielle to start your journey
- Danielle speaking to a group, or a Podcast you would like her to guest speak on
- Booking Danielle to come and facilitate or support an existing team with a team building activity to grow connections in your organization, workplace or club

"I worked through some anger with Danielle that I realized I'd been carrying since childhood. I went in, apprehensive to share. These were deeply embedded emotions, but Danielle created a safe place for me to release . The work I did with her opened up space in me that I had closed off many years ago, and afterwards I felt so much lighter! I also felt an honouring to my own feelings that I had always denied myself. Her guidance and support has been incredibly needed and helpful during a difficult time in my life."

SHERR

Danielle is a gifted group facilitator. She is patient, non-judgemental and kind and holds space so warmly for those working through the assigned activity. I definitely felt a strong, supportive energy from her as I participated in one of her sessions, and this encouraged me to go deeper, and release more. Wow. This woman holds so many gifts. Her own story is inspiring; she normalizes the experience of trauma, understanding that everyone must heal at his/her own pace. Thank you Danielle, and please don't stop this valuable work!

~ MARCY BARBARO, AUTHOR, CO-FOUNDER,
WORKING WRITERS CO.

Metamorphosis might be the right word. Or perhaps transformation. Either way, this is what I witnessed in Danielle as she wrote her book.

Danielle was already full of wisdom when she began the journey of writing her book. As every day progressed, her expression, through her writing, seemed to be awakening the natural energy within her. Just like the caterpillar that transforms into a butterfly, I recall a day when Danielle's essence had shifted. Right in front of the entire class of writers, as she read a section from her developing book, her voice had changed. A power and a calm understanding of what's always resided within was unlocked - just like that. A confidence that was waiting to unveil itself appeared in all its splendor; in all its beauty.

It was an honour to work with Danielle as she wrote her book; an honour to learn from her wisdom, and to appreciate that lives can and do change when you do the work. Congratulations to you, Danielle, as you shine your bright light and guide a new crop of seekers in their respective journeys.

~ ALEX MORIN, CO-CREATOR OF WORKING WRITERS CO.

To learn more, please email danielle@yourconnectioncoach.ca for further details.

ABOUT THE AUTHOR

Danielle is quite familiar moving to the rhythm of 'busy.' She's a married mother of five incredible children ages 28, 26, 22, 17 and 15! All out of her belly, and all on purpose. She's worked as a trauma informed counselor for over 21 years, primarily supporting women experiencing intimate partner abuse. She currently works in the non profit sector facilitating groups for women and youth, and supporting staff with safe space to share and process.

Danielle is a certified fitness trainer who hops on a spin bike weekly running high energy cycling classes. Through past, present and continued work, Danielle keeps embracing a quick pace coupled with an ever present stillness. She's learned there is fluidity in stillness for her that is unique only when stated as such. Danielle finds the more folks she connects with the more they relate to this concept of movement in stillness, and find comfort in it.

Writing this book had Danielle honouring her own story in a way she had been encouraging and holding space for others to do for years. Danielle felt pulled to give back to those who trusted her so implicitly, by placing trust in herself to delve in even deeper and share her journey of tearing down this *Grand Facade*.

After holding a mirror up for countless clients over the years, Danielle chose to turn the mirror on herself, and share with you the fear and pain she hid behind, and how it manifested as body breaks and illness, toxic relationships and a damaging inner narrative.

Connect with her further here:

- Instagram: @dgaucher
- Facebook: Danielle Gaucher

Sometimes the strength within you is not a big fiery flame for all to see it is just a tiny spark that whispers ever so softly "You got this. Keep going."

Manufactured by Amazon.ca
Bolton, ON

32534005R00098